HOW TO WRITE HOT SEX:
Tips from Multi-Published Erotic Romance Authors

Edited by Shoshanna Evers

HOW TO WRITE HOT SEX:
TIPS FROM MULTI-PUBLISHED
EROTIC ROMANCE AUTHORS
Edited by Shoshanna Evers

Visit HowToWriteHotSex.com

ISBN-10: 0991372239
ISBN-13: 978-0-9913722-3-2

DEDICATION

For the love of writing pages that get dog-eared, in books that
remain on readers' bedside tables long after "The End"…

.

CONTENTS

ACKNOWLEDGMENTS

Thank you to the contributors for their enthusiasm and inspiring essays. I learned so much about writing hot sex while editing this book!

Thank you to the fabulous authors who beta-read and reviewed this book. Your time, feedback, and friendship are appreciated and priceless.

Thank you to my first agent for believing in my work, and to the first editor to publish me.

Thank you to my husband, I love you DH!

And most of all, thank you to my readers. Without you I'm just writing into the abyss. Knowing you're there, knowing you're reading, makes it all worthwhile. I love you all from the bottom of my heart. I mean it when I say you can email me anytime. If we're not friends yet, we will be soon!

.

1
PRAISE FOR
HOW TO WRITE HOT SEX

5 stars! "Should be required reading for *all* romance writers! Even non-erotic writers will benefit from the essays in this book. There's something for everyone."
~ Heather Thurmeier, author, heatherthurmeier.com

5 stars! "If you are an erotic romance writer, or are considering writing it, you *need* to read this book. It's jam-packed with information covering all different types of sex scenes. You might want to have a tall glass of ice water handy, too, because even these authors' non-fiction is hot!"
~ Cassandra Carr, author, booksbycassandracarr.com

5 stars! "How to Write Hot Sex is like the Kama Sutra of erotic romance writing, filled with tips and techniques for putting passion and freshness into your sex scenes, whether you write sweet romance or kinky erotica. This how-to book will give you all sorts of "naughty" ideas for turning on your characters and tuning in your readers (and maybe turning them on, too!). Well-known and rising- star erotic romance authors share their personal secrets and tricks of the trade to transform your sex scenes from ho-hum to orgasmic."
~ Cara Bristol, author, carabristol.com

5 stars! "How to Write Hot Sex is a must-have for any aspiring romance writer. The tips from the experienced pros are right on target, along with the blush-worthy excerpts, which demonstrate just how it should be done. Anyone who reads it is guaranteed to walk away with something that will improve their sex scenes. These authors pull no punches and take you from writing something sweet your great-grandmother would approve of to the downright naughty, which will make you blush. There's something in it for everyone!"
~ **Dee Carney,** author, deecarney.com

5 Stars! "How to Write Hot Sex offers practical, smart, nuts-and-bolts writing advice from some of the best erotic romance authors in the business. It's also a fun, sexy, cheeky read—possibly the only sex-writing manual you'll ever need."
~ **Juniper Bell,** author, juniperbell.com

2
INTRODUCTION
BY SHOSHANNA EVERS

How to Write Hot Sex: Tips from Multi-Published Erotic Romance Authors features everything you need to know about adding sizzling sexual tension, scorching sex scenes, and emotional impact to your romance writing in twelve info-packed essays from bestselling and multi-published authors so you can get published and get paid.

Whether you're writing sensual, steamy, or full-on explicit sex scenes, writers can learn from the authors who write and sell sexy books for a living. Do you want to write erotica? Or an erotic romance? Perhaps you just want to add some hot sexual tension to your romance novel.

You've come to the right place.

Here you'll find essays on the art of writing smokin' hot vanilla sex, gay sex, BDSM, kink, and ménage, as well as information on how to find paying markets and publishers for your books and short stories.

How to Write Hot Sex: Tips from Multi-Published Erotic Romance Authors gives you all the information you need to write sex well and get published! The authors are published with New York publishers, small presses, and e-publishers, including Berkley, Simon & Schuster, Kensington, Grand Central Publishing/Forever Yours, Penguin/InterMix, Signet Eclipse,

Ellora's Cave, Harlequin, Carina Press, Samhain, The Wild Rose Press, Loose Id, Flying Pen Press, eXcessiva Publishing, Xcite Books, Circlet Press, loveyoudevine Alterotica, Tirgearr Publishing, Amber Quill Press, Beyond the Page Publishing, Cleis Press, Resplendence Publishing, Totally Bound, Secret Cravings Publishing, Entangled Publishing, as well as becoming Amazon Bestsellers and even *New York Times* and *USA Today* Bestsellers with successfully self-published books.

So what are these gals gonna teach you? We'll start this book off with erotica extraordinaire Cara McKenna, who also writes for Harlequin Blaze as Meg Maguire. Her essay *Real Ugly* will show you how to craft realistic, gritty sex scenes that will raise your prose above "steamy" to "unforgettable." Then we've got the award-winning, prolific Desiree Holt. How prolific? Desiree recently released her one-hundredth book. Now that's what I call multi-published! She shows you how to use all five senses to bring your romance novel to life in *Five Sexy Senses to Rev Up Scenes*.

By now you've probably heard of the huge market for male/male erotic romance. Interestingly, the readership for these stories is mainly straight women. Christine D'Abo teaches you how to cash in on a hot sub-genre with *Boys Will Be Boys: Writing Male/Male Romance*. Then L.K. Below dissects sexual tension in *The Law of Attraction*. With her advice, you'll learn how to make your character's attraction to each other come alive off the page as the sparks fly.

Bestselling Kensington author Kate Douglas (*Wolf Tales*) discusses *Writing the Fine Line Between Erotica and Porn*. By infusing your stories with emotional impact, you'll always have a love story you can be proud of—no matter how explicit or graphic your sex scenes get. You'll learn *How to Write Convincing Fetish and Niche Market Sex* from one of erotica's bestselling LGBT authors, Giselle Renarde. Not sure what all those initials stand for? No worries—Giselle will walk you through the writing process she's perfected over the years in the niche sex erotica market. You won't believe some of the things that could get you on an editor or reader's naughty list. At least you won't be making those mistakes after reading her essay!

Then we get back to the basics with Amazon bestseller Charlotte Stein, who breaks down how to use varying sentence structure and wording to bring your *Sexy Sentences* from drab to fab. Even the hottest story idea won't sell if it's not written well, so heed Charlotte's advice to take your writing to the next level—the level agents, editors, and readers need to see. You can also learn a lot about writing a good sex scene by studying the way fight scenes are written. That's right, fight scenes, like sex scenes, can add levels of intensity and emotion to your stories. Award winning multi-published Isabo Kelly shows you how in her essay *Fighting Sex*.

BDSM erotica is hot—hot to read and hot to sell! Delphine Dryden asks *So You Think You Can Kink?* After reading her essay on Domination and submission in erotic romance, you'll be answering hell yeah I can kink! Then we have *New York Times* bestselling author Jean Johnson, whose essay puts you directly in her classroom as she stands at the podium and plays sexy professor for us in *Biology: The Good, The Bad, & the Sex Scene*. Learning how our bodies physically and mentally become aroused will give you the tools you need to write hot sex with confidence.

But what if you've written a sex scene, and something's just not right? Enter *USA Today* bestseller Cari Quinn and her *Rx for a Sagging Sex Scene*. You'll be able to diagnose an ailing scene and make it exactly the way you need it to be after reading her essay. Lastly, I've contributed an essay on *Getting Published*. In 2010, a year before this book you're reading first came out, Shoshanna Evers didn't exist. In the space of one year I had twelve books release with four different publishers, plus my own self-publishing. I became an Amazon Bestseller with my self-published work, in fact. In the span of one year I went from not existing to leaving my job as an RN to write full time. Now, as of this 2014 updated edition, I'm thrilled to add six books published with Simon & Schuster Pocket Star and the title *New York Times* and *USA Today* Bestselling Author to my name, all thanks to my amazing readers.

If it can happen to me, it can happen for you.

Many authors dream of signing with a literary agency but don't know where to begin—so I decided to share the query letter that snagged my first agent's attention! Everything you need to know about the process of getting published is here. Whether you're hoping to land an agent and multi-book contract with a big New York publisher, write for some of the fabulous electronic publishers, or self-publish and take control of your own publishing destiny, I'll walk you through the steps.

Are you ready? Let's learn *How to Write Hot Sex*! WOOT!

3
REAL UGLY
BY CARA MCKENNA

About Cara McKenna:

Cara McKenna is a multi-published erotic romance author, and also writes steamy contemporary romance as Meg Maguire. She's published with Ellora's Cave, Harlequin, Penguin / InterMix, Samhain, and Signet Eclipse.

#1 *New York Times* bestselling author Maya Banks calls Cara's writing "gritty and compelling."

Before becoming a purveyor of red-hot romance and smart erotica, Cara was a record store bitch, a lousy barista, a decent designer, and an overly enthusiastic penguin handler. Cara now writes full-time and lives north of Boston with her bearded husband.

Real Ugly by Cara McKenna

Imagine a chocolate bar.

Pure, sweet milk chocolate. Pretty good, right? Smooth and rich and creamy…delightful. For a minute or two. Then your taste buds' interest wanes with the even texture, the uniform taste.

Now imagine a chocolate bar you'd bother to tell your friends about. What makes it exceptional? Creaminess is good. But add some dynamism—crunchy toffee or airy nougat, nuts, fruit, or crazy things, like red pepper flakes or coffee beans or lavender. And make it 70% dark chocolate, stone ground for that fascinating, earthy feel. Now *that's* a bar you'd tell a friend about. Not, "I had a chocolate bar. Oh you know, just plain chocolate but it was nice. Real easy to enjoy." *Nice* and *easy* are nice and easy, but *different* is better. Different is worth recommending. "You wouldn't believe the chocolate bar I just tried…"

Erotic romance and erotica, especially, are arguably all about the fantasy. They're escapist genres, and there's nothing wrong with that. They're designed in part to titillate, and again, nothing wrong there. But make the fantasy sex too good, too perfect, too creamy-milk-chocolate, and your reader may set down the book satisfied, but will they remember what they read in a week's time?

Sure, they may. But the scenes I remember (and indeed reread, and re-reread, and sigh wistfully over) are usually chock full of The Ugly. Ugly emotions, imperfect unions, harsh thoughts and words coming from conflicted characters.

I love writing The Ugly. My stories and sex scenes have been called *gritty, real, gut-wrenching, refreshing,* and *train-wreckish.* Greater compliments to me than a mere *steamy.* I'm not afraid to let my characters' sex be imperfect, because I feel the key to creating a compelling fantasy isn't to make everything fantastically perfect. Your sex scenes need to resonate as real, because as lovely as escapism feels, a hint of realism heightens the fantasy from, "Wow, if only sex were really that good!" to "Fuck, that was hot. I wonder if that guy from apartment 8C is into shit like that..."

Put enough of the real into the fantasy, and you'll give readers that sense of *what-if,* that connection that lets them relate to what's happening on the page.

Who Needs Satin When You've Got Sandpaper

How to make sex real, though? You don't need to go overboard. You don't need to include undignified digestive noises, bad breath, ingrown down-there hairs, or spend half a page explaining the enema your character thoughtfully gave him- or herself before submitting to a bit of back-door shenanigans. You don't have to respect biology enough to do the math and figure out when your heroine's going to be getting her monthly visitor (though you could—who knows, it could be hot, if done right).

But do include "ugly" sensory details. Ugly wakes up the reader and keeps them just uncomfortable enough to take the sex from sigh-inducing fantasy to heart-pounding voyeurism (or vicarious exploration, depending on the story and the reader's willingness to *be* the characters, versus *watch* the characters—both are completely valid, incidentally). The ugly—or if you prefer, discordant—elements are what excites the character, author, and reader alike. It wakes you up and roots you in a scene. Makes you read a sentence twice, in a good way. It cleans the Vaseline off the lens and brings it all into focus.

Here are some examples of ugly details. The taste or scent of latex or lubricant on a lover's cock. Bodily fluids accurately (but flatteringly) described—sweat, saliva, come and pre-come, lady-juices, the sting of whiskey still clinging to a lover's lips. The horrible realization that she wore her grodiest underwear and didn't shave her legs, not having expected to get laid (starts with embarrassment, ends with abandon). The sting of a slap or a sweet-nothing that triggers a bad memory. The coolness and grit of a hardwood floor under her back, the friction of the cheap carpet burning his knees, the awkwardness and exposure of a backseat. The scrape of nails and teeth. The ache in the jaw and gag in the throat during oral. The challenges of pairing a tall character with the short one, a beautiful one with an insecure one. The intimidating sensation of large man's weight, and your character's fear they may not be able to handle his physicality, his cock, his words, his kinks, or his distance and indifference when the sun comes up the next morning. The gracelessness of a man as he goes beyond the bounds of coordination, self-control and perfection, giving way to the erratic, frantic slap of skin on skin as his cock calls the shots.

Don't Be Afraid to Interrupt

Keeping with the imperfection of reality, a bump in the action adds the valley that makes the peaks surrounding it all the more exciting, spiking the longing and impatience in both the characters and reader.

However, it can't be as generic as an arbitrary phone call. If the sex is so hot, why would the heroine bother answering it? But if it were her ex-lover's personalized ringtone…hmmm. There's an interesting reversal. Don't interrupt every sex scene, obviously, but don't hesitate to call a time-out and let reality intrude.

If you're a brave author who doesn't gloss over the issue of birth control and safe sex, don't be afraid to let that damn condom slow things down. It feels like an unsexy moment, that annoying, obligatory formality hijacking the fantasy. But let it! Let lube-slick fingers fumble with the wrapper. Let the characters get frustrated. Let that moment show the heroine (or hero) that the guy cares, or let the hero see that the woman he's with isn't afraid to lay down the law and make demands. Let her carry her own damn condoms. Let them realize neither remembered protection and force them to get creative, saving penetration for next time. Oooh, next time.

Also, don't forget to prep. As I said before, you don't have to drag the reader along for the enema, if your character's a thoughtful and hygienic anal recipient. But please—no ramming it up a character's back-end without lubricant or at least spit, without the preparation of fingers or glacially-slow penetration. Don't omit lube from a scene because you think your heroine's pussy has to be enough, each and every time. Don't shy from the real.

Don't Be Afraid of Fail-Sex

So as we've covered, even fantasy sex should be imperfect. Imperfect is real, and real is resonant, accessible and compelling. Taking that idea a bit further still, don't be afraid to let a sex act "fail". Have you ever actually had sex using whipped cream or frosting or other food stuffs? It's a mess. Sex on the beach? Good for you. Still finding sand where the sun don't shine? Leave your characters laughing about their attempt to spice things up, then send them to the shower to redeem the evening.

One area in particular I feel needs more failure is threesomes. What a powder keg that dynamic *should* be, especially if two of the lovers are committed or established! So often, one character wants it more than another. Oooh, that's good. Go with that. I've written both angry three-ways, such as the ones in *Shivaree* and *Ready and Willing*, where at least one character consented under duress or out of fear (though they pretended they were fine with the idea—they weren't cruelly coerced), and one ménage that plain old failed (*Ruin Me*) when the third decided he just wasn't going there and walked out at the height of the festivities. I've also written three-ways that started out "Oh God, what am I doing?" and ended up mind-blowing. And three-ways that started as a favor to one character, and wound up instilling their indulgent partner with a profound sense of satisfaction from being the one who let that fantasy be realized (both *Don't Call Her Angel* and *Dirty Thirty*). Fuck with the power dynamics. Oh, the power dynamics…

Rock that Boat

First and foremost, when writing hot sex, keep it edgy. And

by "edgy" I don't mean tossing in handcuffs or anal or spanking or any other kinky extra. Edgy means the reader and characters are *on edge*. Turned on, but perhaps not entirely comfortable with how turned on they are.

As examples of discomfort-as-spice, I've written stories about a heroine scared but curious about exploring her lover's rape fantasy kink (*Willing Victim*), a married man finally indulging his need to have sex with another man (*Dirty Thirty*), more than one hesitant heroine finally letting a man get close to her (one a virgin, one a stranger to orgasm) and a militantly straight guy falling for another man for the first time in his life, thoroughly against his will (the entire *Shivaree* series). It's all about that internal back-and-forth. "I don't want to want this, but I do. But I can't act on it, because acting on it would change how I see myself, and how this other person sees me. But crap, I really want to…" Tortured characters are a joy to write and read about, as long as you don't manifest their torment as a never-ending swathe of lamenting introspection.

Ultimately, of course, curiosity will trump fear, but the conflict doesn't end when consent is tendered.

When I write erotica, I don't saddle myself with the burden of plot. A simple situation sets the stage (a single woman decides she wants to enlist men to help her conceive a baby the good old-fashioned way; young marrieds source a third for their first m/m/f threesome) and that's all you need. A situation poses a question: what will happen if they go through with this? No bad guy to apprehend, no family business to save, merely an experience to explore.

Erotica is so sex-centric, plot dilutes a shorter story, as backward as that sounds. Make a book too much about a traditional plot, and the sex will feel crowbarred in, or vice versa. It's a sex book, and that's plenty. That's legitimate. Sex is fascinating, and there's no need to dress it up. Let sex drive the story, not some half-baked suspense yarn that gets tied up in a hurry after the fifth boinking session. It's the emotions at play that constitute the conflict, both internal and between the various characters, in the absence of an external plot. Will they regret it? Who's got the power? Is one person being indulged, the other under duress? Will it bring them closer or drive them apart?

I can't think of any emotion more exciting than *misgiving*. Misgiving, be it fear, jealousy, shame, or doubt, means there's something at stake, an imbalance in power, hopefully one that shifts in different scenarios. Think about it: a teeter-totter in motion in infinitely more exciting that a perfectly balanced one, or one permanently anchored on one end. As fun as power-play is, keeping it fluid and "fair" is important, too.

In *Backwoods*, (the first book in the series about the straight guy, Shane, who's been seduced by another man, Gabriel) Shane feels as though he's going out of his mind, finding himself drawn to do things he doesn't want to want…but Gabriel is equally vulnerable, because his feelings are hurt by Shane's need to hide what they've become. Shane's ashamed— borderline disgusted—by what they do, while what they've become means everything to Gabriel. Ouch.

In a ménage I wrote where a woman gets permission from her boyfriend to sleep with a man she's been obsessed with for years (*Ruin Me*), the heroine seems to have all the power. She's getting what she wants, though it violates the bounds of her primary relationship. But her boyfriend has power, too—the power to offer her the freedom to do what she needs to, and also the power to dictate exactly how far that leash extends.

Similarly, in another ménage of mine, *Don't Call Her Angel*, the wife seems on the outside to be the powerless one—her husband is brutish and rough, selfish and demanding in bed. But everything he does is actually a realization of his wife's submissive kinks. And when he allows her to realize her fantasy of bringing another man into their bed, the power seems to be all hers. The husband is, after all, almost painfully conservative and controlling. But underneath her fantasy is his own—the desire to be the man with the power to grant her every wish.

In another story I paired a virgin heroine with a male prostitute hero (*Curio*). Now there's a funky match. A sexual know-nothing versus a man who fucks for money. But she's the one paying and calling all the shots, which again ushers in that pleasantly rickety power balance.

Keep the control in constant flux and ride that delightful edge of discomfort, and also surprise your readers by letting your characters' internal identities contradict their shells here and there. If one character seems from the outside to hold all the obvious power, make sure that a few layers beneath that, they may actually be the desperate one. Conversely, make sure the vulnerable one is holding some cards of his or her own, and let the balance shift, keeping everyone on edge. Comfort is the enemy of excitement. Don't give it a foothold.

DIY Bondage

I just wanted to include this final section for fun. Hot on the heels of all that talk of power dynamics, let's touch on BDSM.

Some people would say I write BDSM—my characters frequently have rough sex and my heroes often skew bossy and domineering. Those are BDSM themes, but I wouldn't claim to write true BDSM. BDSM is a set of sexual conventions (no matter how unconventional), some might say an organized subculture, with quite a lot of social protocol underpinning it all. I'm not an expert on the scene in any way, but it brings to mind for me the "dungeon" tableau, costumes of the latex and leather varieties, the uttering of "Sir" and "Mistress" and "slave", elaborate role playing, and the fetishization of power to the nth degree. It's an extremely popular and utterly valid sub-sub-genre of erotic romance, but I'm not drawn to that incarnation of BDSM. Too much pomp and circumstance, too much scene-setting for my authorly and readerly taste. I'll leave that to the folks who do it well and know what they're talking about.

But I frequently write what I like to call "DIY (do-it-yourself) bondage". Accessible, even spontaneous instances of power-play kink that you could imagine happening to everyday people.

My characters aren't the types to have cuffs and Velcro safety restraints lying around. When they get kinky, it's not planned and accessorized. They tie each other down with belts and pantyhose and folded-over duct tape. They may have safe words, because that's just a responsible portrayal of respectfully orchestrated Dom/sub type sex, but there's no "yes, Master" uttered in my books. No floggers, no ball-gags, no hot wax drippage, no collars.

If you're like me and you love to explore power dynamics but don't care for the hardcore bondage accoutrements, rest assured you can write filthy-nasty-awesome D/s sex without a single BDSM prop. Your character isn't the type to own a fuck-swing, you say? Well does he have a bathroom counter of roughly hip-height? Can't see him leading her around on a leash? How about a mean fist tangled in her hair as he steers her toward the bed? Who needs leather straps, when there's nothing sexier than being held down by a strong man's bare hands? In short, get creative, go minimalist. It all feeds back to that point about the spice of realism.

And of Course...

Write what turns you on. That doesn't mean it's anything you'd ever want to try out yourself, and you can't paralyze yourself, fretting if people will think your erotic novella about Smurf-kink is autobiographical. They say write what you know, but in erotica, imagination is just as important as experience. I mean, I've never established my own harem, or had sex with a boxer, a lumberjack, or a Parisian man-whore, but it sure as hell didn't stop me from writing those stories.

Do what so many articles and books advise, and don't worry about your mom or kid or pastor reading your work. You aren't your characters, and even if others may not realize that, you can't let it inhibit you. Don't hold back. Readers can sense self-conscious and self-censored sex-writing as easily as they can spot a typo.

Happy readers are never guaranteed, with one exception: you can write a book that absolutely and utterly turns *you* on.

So there's one satisfied reader, and I promise you, if you give it everything you have and reduce your own legs to jelly, others will feel it, too. But here's another guarantee: water down the words and scenes you fear are too racy, too kinky, too out-there, and you may merely be the first of many readers who feel cheated, or bored, or *meh*.

Always remember: it's far better to inspire a debate than a nap. So get your ass on the chair and your fingers on the keyboard, and keep yourself on edge.

Cara McKenna wants you to stay in touch!

Website: caramckenna.com
Blog: wonkomance.com/author/cara/
Tumblr: superluckyfun.tumblr.com/
Twitter: twitter.com/caramckenna
Goodreads: goodreads.com/caramckenna
Email: cara@caramckenna.com

4

FIVE SEXY SENSES TO REV UP SCENES
BY DESIREE HOLT

About Desiree Holt

Desiree Holt is an award-winning multi-published erotic romance author. She's been published with Ellora's Cave, Totally Bound, The Wild Rose Press, Samhain Publishing, Decadent Publishing and Secret Cravings Publishing.

She is twice a finalist for an EPIC E-Book Award (and a winner in 2014), a nominee for a Romantic Times Reviewers Choice Award, winner of the first 5 Heart Sweetheart of the Year Award at The Romance Studio as well as twice a CAPA Award for best BDSM book of the year, and winner of two Holt Medallion Awards. She has been featured on *CBS Sunday Morning* and in *The Village Voice*, *The Daily Beast*, *USA Today* and numerous other national publications.

Reviewers call Desiree "a force to be reckoned with in the erotic romance department!" and "the most amazing erotic romance author of our time." USA Today calls her "The Nora Roberts of erotic romance.)

Desiree has a weakness for hot cowboys and men on motorcycles. She's also an obsessed football addict.

Five Sexy Senses to Rev Up Scenes
by Desiree Holt

Okay, the hero and heroine have met. They've had that first electric moment. They've teased each other and stroked each other, all the while knowing that at any moment they were going to *have sex!*

Of course the anticipation is half of it. Light nibbling kisses followed by deep ones with tongues gliding against each other. Erotic words murmured in low voices. Touching each other here and there. Until holding back becomes unbearable.

So how do you get into it without looking like you're just following a direction that says *"Insert sex here?"*

For one thing, you have to get in the mood. Don't write sex when the kids are squabbling or you're in between loads of laundry or making a list of errands. Lots of things can get you in the mood. A glass of wine. Soft music. A satin sleep shirt (not kidding here!). But most of all you have to use your imagination.

Think yourself into the scene. Why is the heroine in bed with the hero? What drew them together? What is their connection? In *Once Upon a Wedding* my heroine wanted one last fling before getting married and on a sunset beach she found Joe, who knew all the secret ways to please a woman. It's as much what he says as what he does.

***

"Your mouth tastes like a rare wine, Rainie." He whispered his words into her open lips. "I'll bet your cunt tastes even better."

Moisture flooded her panties at his words. She swallowed her hesitation and asked, "Are you going to find out?"

"Oh, yes. You bet your sweet ass I am. In more ways than you can count." He stepped back from her. His hand came up and traced the outline of her jaw, the shell of her ear, the slender column of her neck. "The minute I saw you sitting on that beach I wanted to rip your clothes off and fuck you senseless."

Her mouth formed a small *O*.

***

So you have to think about what you'd like the hero to say if it was you in that bed with him.

You also need to focus on the best tools for sex. No, not toys! The five senses.

You get there by using the five senses: touch, see, hear, smell and taste. In every scene there are things that each of these responds to. Oh, and don't forget to use adjectives that evoke images in the reader's mind.

Touch.

Him: her small hands were nearly swallowed up by his large ones as he reached for her breasts. Her skin was the softest silk, smooth beneath his fingers. **Her**: She could feel the roughness of his hands, the callouses from hard work just slightly abrading her skin and sending shivers along her spine.

See.

Him: He looked at her standing there, backlit by the fire blazing in the fireplace, her hair a burnished gold in the reflected light. He could see every dip and swell of her body. She couldn't tear her eyes away from him. **Her**: He looked like a Norse warrior towering over her with his thick head of golden hair, his fierce blue eyes, his broad back and his sculptured muscles. His swollen cock pressing against the zipper of his jeans.

Hear.

Him: His name on her lips was like sweet music, her laugh the sound of wind chimes. It made his balls tingle and his dick want to push itself inside her. **Her**: His voice was low and deep, a sound that rumbled through her as he spoke her name like a caress.

Smell.

Him: As he bent his head toward hers he inhaled her scent, a heady mixture of jasmine and fresh rain. **Her**: She caught the scent of his soap and aftershave, a combination of spice and earth and musk. The pulse in her pussy throbbed with a hungry need to feel him inside her.

Taste.

Him: Her lips were so soft beneath his and when they opened for him his tongue swept inside. She tasted like chocolate and fine wine, a taste that went straight to his groin and fired every nerve in his body. **Her**: When his tongue tangled with hers she was reminded of the taste of cinnamon and whiskey, a very masculine combination that made her body soften and her pulses throb.

Notice that I'm also not afraid to give explicit names to various parts of the anatomy. Don't be afraid of them. Just the sound of them is titillating to the reader. And describing how they each appear to the other hooks the reader into what's happening and makes the actual sex vividly emotional.

Some scenes need a setup and that's where the combination of physical and emotional comes in. Like in this scene from *Down and Dirty*:

***

His hands came up to cup her face as his head bent and his mouth covered hers. His hands set up tingles in the skin of her cheeks and the touch of his lips sent sparks of sensation showering through her. Her breasts suddenly felt full and moisture flooded the crotch of her thong. He nibbled at her lower lip, teasing at it, tugging it between his teeth. Krista clutched his wrists, unable to do more than hang on and hope she didn't fall. When she opened her mouth on a sigh, his tongue moved inside without hesitation, brushing every interior surface, the tip of his tongue tracing lines against the roof of her mouth.

His body moved fractionally against her, enough that his legs bracketed her and the hardness of his cock pushed at her through his jeans. Heat consumed her, the walls of her pussy vibrated and she couldn't have pushed him away to save herself.

When he lifted his head, she was dazed and breathless, her eyes held captive by those unusual silver ones, now darkening to a stormy grey. His tongue swiped lightly across her mouth.

"I think we need to take this somewhere a little more private, don't you?"

***

But once you take it "somewhere a little more private," don't be afraid to be explicit. Again, rely on the five senses. What does each of them feel? Taste? See? And so on.

Sometimes in a book I jump right into the sex but only because there is a specific reason for it. In *Jungle Inferno,* my hero Mark is a prisoner of terrorists in the Peruvian jungle while Faith, the woman he loves, is a continent away for most of the book. I mean, the guy's got an impressive cock but it doesn't reach across thousands of miles, right? So how to get them together? How to show the reader their intense physical connection in a way that's not jarring? I solved it by opening with a hot sex scene. Mark is in a tent, wounded and filthy and in pain and the only thing keeping him sane is his fantasies about Faith.

***

It was raining, a steady thrumming on the broad leaves of the trees and plants that formed a thick canopy over the jungle floor. By the time it reached the thick carpet of dead plants and rotting wood it was more like a mist, a thick curtain of steam that sat heavily on the skin.

Mark Halloran inhaled deeply, the sweet scent of vanilla and sarsaparilla plants mingling with that of the wild orchids. The dense rainforest of the Peruvian jungle held a wild mixture of flora whose perfume teased at the senses and conjured up images. Beneath the heavier perfume of these and other plants like cinchona and cedar, was the vague hint of the abundance of orchids growing in wild profusion.

But none so arousing as the scent of the woman in his arms. Light jasmine drifted from the silken fall of her hair and mingled with the sweetness of her body. And the musk of her arousal. He ran his hand over the satiny surface of her skin, feeling every dip and hollow with the tips of his fingers. The indentation of her navel. The crease where hip and thigh joined. The soft bush of the curls covering her cunt.

Bending his head he pulled a dusky nipple into his mouth, swirling his tongue around it before pressing it flat against the roof of his mouth. He was rewarded with a soft moan and an arching of Faith's body that pushed the nipple deeper into his mouth. His hand molded the full swell of her breast, loving the feel of its weight in his palm.

His cock had been hard enough to drive nails from the moment they'd entered the tent that had been pitched for them. A jungle vacation with as many amenities as the rainforest had to offer. They'd nearly ripped their clothes in the urgency to get rid of them, to feel naked skin against naked skin. So many months had passed since they'd been together that he was afraid he'd come before they even got started.

You're Special Ops, asshole. You have legendary control. Use it now. So he'd gritted his teeth and dialed it back as much as he could, willing himself to take the time to do this properly.

But just looking at her was enough to ramp up his simmering arousal. Her naked body was a work of art, lush hips and breasts, long legs and at the juncture of her thighs the soft nest of curls that hid the mysteries of her sex—the sweetest cunt he'd ever tasted or fucked. A wet heat that scorched him, drowned him with the liquid of her passion. His only conflict was whether to fuck her first with his mouth or his cock. He'd barely contained himself enough to urge her down to the mat with him, so great was the need to take her where they stood.

He moved his mouth to the other nipple, poking at him so temptingly, and trailed his hand down her body over the soft swell of her tummy to the wet slit of her pussy. God, she was always so wet for him so quickly. How was he supposed to hold back?

Faith opened her thighs to his touch and his thumb easily found the hot nub of her clitoris. As he pulled deeply on her taut nipple his thumb brushed back and forth against the tiny bundle of nerves, drawing the little cries of pleasure from her that turned him on so much.He lifted his head to brush his lips against hers, gently licking the seam of her lips, teasing at the corners, nipping lightly on the full lower one. He'd always been fascinated by the sensuous swell of those lips, loved kissing them and tasting them. Nipping on them. He thought he could spend hours just making love to her mouth.

When she opened them he slipped his tongue inside, scraping over the edge of her teeth to find the hot slickness of the skin inside. The touch of her small tongue against his sent arrows of heat jolting through him, straight to his throbbing cock and his aching balls.

Slow, asshole. Slow. Show her how much you appreciate her. How you feel about her.

He danced with her tongue, darting back and forth over its surface while his thumb continued to work her clit in a slow, steady motion. Faith moaned again, the tight little sound echoing into his own mouth. Her hands pressed against his back, pulling him down closer to her.

When she bent her legs, planting her feet firmly on the woven mat, a silent invitation to explore farther, he moved his hand until he could slide two fingers into the hot well of her cunt.

Oh, god. *Hot!* Hot, hot, hot!

She was so very wet, the walls of her pussy slippery with her juices, her flesh pulsing against his fingers.

He tore his mouth away from her.

"I can't wait any longer." His voice was so hoarse he didn't even recognize it.

"Then don't," she urged. "It's been so long. I'm ready for you. Now."

Mark reached for the foil packet he'd dropped beside them, ripped it open with his teeth and extracted the latex sheath. Levering himself to his knees he deftly rolled it on with one hand, ready for action.

But the sight of her wet, welcoming, pink pussy was so tempting, so mouth-watering, that first he had to have a taste. He lowered his head, spread her labia wide with his thumbs and lapped the length of her slit.

"Ohhhhh."

The long exhalation of pleasure sent another surge of heat through him. God, he loved those sounds. So he did it again. And again. Until he wasn't sure exactly who he was teasing. Licking the sweet-tart taste of her from his lips, he positioned himself, pressing the head of his cock at the opening of her vagina and with one hard roll of his hips he entered her wet heat.

Oh, Jesus!

The walls of her cunt clamped around him and it was like being burned alive with the sweetest heat. He gritted his teeth, every muscle in his body tightening with the need for release, but he held himself still, giving himself time to enjoy the feel of her like a hot glove around him.

***

This is an example of a scene that uses the senses—everything Mark is feeling. What goes through his mind and how his body reacts as he sees every part of her. I put the reader in Mark's mind and pulled her into the scene. Using the five senses. Remember that if you remember nothing else. *THE FIVE SENSES.*

These are just a few examples of how to fit hot sex into a book without it being editorial and how to make it come alive for your readers. Remember. Think it. Feel it. Describe it. Don't be afraid of it. Call up your most secret fantasies. Who is the man of your dreams? If you were alone with him—

naked—what would you want him to do to you? *With* you? Take another sip of that wine and let your imagination run wild.

And the scenes you write will singe your computer.

Desiree Holt wants you to stay in touch!
Website: www.desireeholt.com
Blog: www.desireeholttellsall.com
Twitter: www.twitter.com/desireeholt
Facebook: www.facebook.com/desireeholt
Goodreads: www.goodreads.com/desireeholt
Email: desireeholt@desireeholt.com

5
BOYS WILL BE BOYS:
WRITING MALE/MALE ROMANCE
BY CHRISTINE D'ABO

About Christine d'Abo:

Christine d'Abo is a multi-published erotic romance author. She's been published with Carina Press/Harlequin, Cleis Press, Ellora's Cave and Forever Yours.

Reviewers have called Christine's writing, "...more passionate than the one before and will leave you breathless in the end. Ms. d'Abo definitely knows her stuff!"

Christine started writing m/m romance when she got annoyed when her favorite TV show didn't give her the happily ever after she wanted to see. When Christine isn't writing, she's watching sci-fi shows or exercising in her basement.

Boys Will Be Boys:
Writing Male/Male Romance
by Christine D'Abo

In The Beginning

A few years ago when I penned the final line on my book No Quarter, my husband asked if I needed him to proofread it for me. He has always been one of my biggest supporters and loves to help when and where he can. I turned and gave him a *look*. I know this because he gave me his answering *look*, rolled his eyes and asked, "What the hell did you write this time?"

"Umm, a male/male space opera."

"Why?"

"Because the hero I had in mind turned out to be gay?" I may have shrugged. I believe there was eye-rolling on the part of my husband.

It was odd, but I hadn't considered giving my hero Gar a female counterpoint at any stage in the writing of the story. For me the decision to enter the area of m/m romance wasn't something I'd strategically planned out. I went where my characters took me—in this case, Gar led me to Faolan.

If you are considering trying your hand at writing gay romance, then you need to pick a few of the top names and read. Pick different styles, genres, stories written by gay men and straight women. Explore all you are able to find, and try to discover what elements you enjoy as a reader.

In general, I feel the biggest mistake new writers to erotic romance make (regardless of whether it's hetero- or homosexual), is the focus they initially place on *sex*. Yes, the sex is a necessary component and if written poorly, it detracts from an otherwise enjoyable story. But it's not the heart of what's happening. Like traditional romance, erotic romance focuses on the journey of two (or more) people (aliens/werewolves/vampires/whatever) while they figure out

27

who they are in life and how their heart factors into these events.

Sex is the mechanism by which the writer shows these characters at their best and worst in their journey. Each sex scene needs to be treated as a connected character development ladder, running parallel to the plot points driving your hero to change. A successful erotic writer builds on each sexual encounter, using the growing closeness and the stripped emotional state of the characters to expose their weaknesses. Once this is done, you are ready to shove them into the pit of their black moment where they must confront their fears or die.

Wait, wasn't this supposed to be about male/male romance?

It is!

One of the things I've often noticed as a reader is how sometimes, in a story I'm reading, the sex feels like it has been added as an afterthought, like the writer made a footnote in their draft that stated, "Add sex here." I've particularly noticed this in many male/male romances. I'm not sure if this has to do with the uncertainty some authors have in the execution of the actual sex act on paper, or if it's a matter of style. I suspect it might be a bit of both.

I'm going to attempt to sketch out how I go about the writing a successful male/male sex scene. Like all advice on writing, everything won't necessarily work for every person. Take what makes sense to you and use it, change it up and make it your own.

Boy Bits

For the record, I love men. It's not exactly a hardship for me to write a story about two broken, beautiful, well-endowed men and put them together in a romantic relationship. No, I'm not a gay man. No, I've never had to live with the emotional or societal struggles that a gay man faces. I'm also not an alien, time-traveling steampunk heroine, a soldier or a coffee shop owner.

Like it is in any kind of writing, research in male/male romance is important. Yes, that includes research into sexual practices as well. You will need to know what frottage is, rimming, fisting, blowjobs, where the prostate is, what someone's first time bottoming is like, what the hell "bottoming" *means*...I'll go through some of these terms in a few moments. There's also lube to consider, positions, safe sex, when and why someone wouldn't participate in safe sex, and everything else you could possibly imagine.

You need to be comfortable with these concepts and understand why someone would choose (or not choose) to do something of a sexual nature. This is the same for heterosexual erotic romance as well, and generally a good rule for any element you want to incorporate into a story. Every act needs a purpose within the narrative or character development arc, and is a potential source of conflict. For example: Maybe one of your heroes won't give blow jobs. It could be that he's convinced it makes him less of a man. Over the course of the sex scenes, your hero will have to come to terms with his issues and by the end of the story, he'll have to be willing to at least give the act a shot. By the time you get to the scene where he actually goes down on his lucky partner, that simple act will have a great deal of meaning for the characters, beyond just the sex and sensuality.

You need to make sure you keep the boy bits straight. Yes, I understand the irony of that statement. Make sure your research includes getting very familiar with the mechanics of how testicles and penises work; those are the kinds of details that your characters would logically know and make use of during sex. It's also important to understand some of the wonderful sexual positions men can get up to with each other, so don't forget to research that as well. In any erotic romance, variety is the spice of life. Change things up for your characters while pushing their comfort levels. You'll want to have each sexual encounter built on some element, bringing them closer to that black moment and resolution.

Keeping the boy bits straight is also a matter of keeping

your pronouns straight, because you don't want your reader confused about who is doing what to whom. One of the biggest challenges I faced when I first started writing No Quarter was the over-use of names in sex scenes. When you can't rely on using he/him/his (since there is more than one "him") it's tempting to always use first names; however, that makes the writing stilted, so you have to come up with ways around it. One of the tricks I fell back on for that book was keeping the sex scene clearly in one character's point of view. This helped ensure that I didn't over-use the names and could rely on pronouns more.

You may also have some initial challenges in the description of the actual sex acts, keeping the arms, legs and cocks of your heroes straight. If you can't visualize what it is they are doing, you may want to consider having a picture or video available to you as you write the scene, to help clarify who or what is going where. Yes, I do enjoy my research.

Boys Will Be Boys

For the record, a gay man is not a woman. I mean, *of course* a gay man isn't a woman. He's generally got a cock, which is a dead giveaway in my books. I'm a woman, not a gay man...and while we may both have the same love and appreciation for the male body, that doesn't mean our outlooks are the same.

My biggest gripe with some of the male/male romances I've read is around the feminization of some of the men in the story. This is a trap that female writers of gay romance can easily slip into. It's something I had to watch myself when I was writing No Remedy. I had a very alpha male who was one-third of a romantic m/m/f triad. I kept trying to slip my beta male into a more feminine role, despite the fact I had a heroine as well.

While gay men and women do have similar outlooks on certain aspects of life, there are differences. I'm stating the obvious, but it's an easy thing to forget. There are a number of documentaries out there a writer can watch (The Making of Me, TransGeneration, both pop to mind) to get a better understanding of some of the fundamental differences between homosexuality and heterosexuality. The world isn't black and white though, so be comfortable exploring different ideas and be careful to avoid slipping into clichés.

Not all gay men are fashion designers. Nor are they all big fans of musical theatre. They don't all don't cry at the drop of a hat; they are not all in tune with their feminine side. They are still men.

In my writing, I've had some of my male characters be bisexual, though in the story they are only engaged in a homosexual relationship. I do this because I love the added layer of complexity it adds to that individual. It also forces me to avoid some of the typical clichés that I might be drawn to use, because the characters don't readily fit into any of the gay male stereotypes. A great example of an against-type gay hero is one of the most complex heroes on television, Captain Jack Harkness from Doctor Who and Torchwood. He's not gay or bi – he's omnisexual. Yes, Jack will sleep with anything!

Understanding what some of the terms and clichés are will help you avoid them. If you understand them well enough, you can take them and turn them on their heads, helping you to advance your plot and further your character growth.

Here are a few terms you may have heard used:

Twink - A younger, attractive, boyish gay man. Usually one who is thin and preppy looking. Young, shallow and cute.

Bear - Bearded man, usually somewhat stouter than the average man, with or without body hair. Term was created by men who felt that mainstream gay culture was unwelcoming to men who did not fit a particular "twink" body norm.

Queen - An effeminate boy or man. The stereotypical effeminate homosexual. The term is not ordinarily applied to the virile, masculine sort of homosexual.

Those are some of the "flavors" of homosexual man, types we're all familiar with. While these stereotypes do exist in real life, I personally try to avoid them in my writing. It's too much like taking the easy way out, which is something we should always avoid; even if you start there when you first picture your character, you need to transcend those ideas as you flesh that character out.

Remember that a person is more than just a sexual orientation. Doctors, lawyers, auto mechanics, engineers, soldier, space explorers...the profession isn't reliant on the character's sexuality. Just as you must consider the whole story before focusing on the sex, consider the whole character before focusing on the sexuality; while aspects of sex and sexual preference may be integral, they can't be the sole foundation on which you build your story, even when you're writing m/m erotica.

A final note on stereotyping: *gay* doesn't necessarily mean *kinky*. The appeal of kink is different and doesn't always translate over to a gay romance. If there is a reason for the kink to be added to the story, then ensure you've done your research on the nature, impact and psychological reasons behind the kink. But don't assume that because a character is gay, he'll automatically be knowledgeable about, or a participant in, the BDSM aspects of the "leather" lifestyle.

Bottoms Up!

Okay, on to the good stuff: writing the actual sex scene!

There is a lot of information out there on positions. There is more than just doggie style. Be creative! Do some research to learn more about what people can get up to. Learn the terminology, too. In erotic romance, you can't be afraid of calling a cock a cock. No flowery euphemisms should be used. Likewise, don't over-use the pet names, cute phrases or anything that will pull the reader out of the story.

Here are a few vocabulary terms to get you started.

Catching - The one who is to be penetrated in an anal sex act. (the penetrating partner is the "pitcher").

Rimming - The act of licking or sucking the anus of a sex partner, lubricating it with saliva, usually as a prelude to fucking his anus; widening the partner's anus with the tongue.

Frottage - Frottage is a term for phallus-against-phallus sex, where two guys put their hard cocks together and rub and grind till they shoot. You can frot in a bearhug, or lying down, or by gripping both cocks in one fist.

Cowboy – The man on top is penetrated and rides his partner. Person on top sets the pace.

When I'm plotting out the sex, I will start with a fairly basic first encounter; again, the character development is central, not the logistics of the sex act itself. I love a good emotional struggle on the part of at least one of the men before they consent to sex. It can be fun to have at least one of the men feel as if this is a onetime deal that they will be able to walk away when everything is done. This is often referred to as the "gay for you" dynamic. That makes the second sex scene that much more emotionally charged and opens up the potential for one of your heroes to start to show cracks in his emotional armor.

In Pulled Long (book three in my Long Shots series), Ian is a gay man who has fallen for a customer. Ian and Jeff explore the benefits and pitfalls of exhibitionism. As a writer, this gave me many options for exploring Ian's backstory by examining what drove him to wanting to do this in the first place. It also gave me a wide variety of positions and places where they could have fun. The sex in that story becomes the catalyst for the black moment; the breakup of Jeff and Ian. Ian is forced to face his fears of abandonment or else run the risk of losing Jeff forever.

Gar, one of my heroes in No Quarter, has cut himself off from as much human contact as possible. Faolan uses sex as a way of breaking through Gar's emotional barriers, helping him deal with his traumatic past while giving him hope for the future. Their scenes had a Domination/submission dynamic as well, which added tension to interactions but also helped establish Faolan as a strong, trustworthy caretaker of Gar's affections.

Give your sex scenes as much physical detail as you are able, while keeping the emotional descriptions active throughout. By melding the two together, the scene will have more of an impact and stay with your readers longer.

In the End

One of the things I've chosen to do as a writer is not deal with societal issues that gay men face. This is a conscious decision on my part, as I don't feel comfortable dealing with those. I'd rather explore the human condition, those challenges that many of us face on a daily basis, using sex as the means to do so.

You are a different person, a different writer with experiences well outside of my own. Use what you know, talk to friends and family to get a perspective on what it is you wish to show. Once you have the emotions of that particular issue, you'll find the sex will pack more of a punch when your characters are finally ready to do the deed.

Christine D'Abo wants you to stay in touch!
Website: www.christinedabo.com
Tumblr: http://christinedabo.tumblr.com/
Twitter: twitter.com/Christine_dAbo
Facebook: facebook.com/Author.Christine.dAbo
Goodreads: .
goodreads.com/author/show/2737770.Christine_d_Abo
Email: christine.dabo@gmail.com

6
THE LAW OF ATTRACTION
BY L.K. BELOW

About L.K. Below:

L.K. Below is a multi-published erotic romance author. She's been published with Liquid Silver Books, Cliffhanger Books, Breathless Press, Lyrical Press, Inc. and MuseItHot Publishing, Inc.

Reviewers have said L.K. Below's writing "epitomizes everything I love about romance" and invokes a passion that "leaps off the page."

L.K. is a self-proclaimed nerd and bookworm. Chances are if you can't find her writing a book, you'll find her with her nose in one!

The Law of Attraction by L.K. Below

What attracts one person to another? Every person—every character—has his or her own tastes. This fundamental fact has led to sayings such as "Beauty is in the eye of the beholder." But is it really? Depends on who you ask.

The standard of beauty throughout the ages has changed drastically. Let's rewind to the medieval era, when to be considered beautiful you just needed to have all your teeth. Unblemished skin was a bonus. In ages past, heavier women were considered beautiful for the same reason as those with teeth— it suggested they had a more comfortable style of living.

These days, nothing so dire contributes to the standard of beauty. It's still desirable for a woman to have all her teeth, but heavier weight no longer plays an essential role, because it's no longer a reflection on the standard of living. As a result, beauty has undergone a drastic change.

Does that mean your heroine has to be thin, leggy, and blonde?

Absolutely not. Men all have their tastes. Some men are ass men, some prefer a woman's legs, some like breasts. Similarly, different men prefer different body types.

So what attracts two people to each other?

Several studies have shown that symmetry is key. Not only body symmetry, but facial symmetry as well. Since beauty is in the eye of the beholder, everyone holds his own standard of physical beauty and his own ideas of traits or physical flaws which can be overlooked in a partner. Noted psychologists such as Sigmund Freud and Carl Jung have even gone so far to infer that men and women choose partners with the idealized traits of their mothers and fathers.

Sir Isaac Newton was the first to suggest a Law of Attraction in science. In *Opticks*, he suggested that "likes attract likes". Water will be attracted to water, air to air, and so on. This concept has also been applied to relationships. Often men and women choose partners of a similar social background, upbringing, religion, interests, and even of a similar level of attractiveness.

But what about the old saying "opposites attract"? Does that also hold true? Many social psychologists believe it does. While men and women choose partners with similar values, they often choose complementary or polar opposites in terms of personality. The Dominant/submissive relationship is a perfect example. A submissive person by nature will continually seek someone naturally dominant.

Okay—what does this have to do with sex?

In a word: *everything*. Sex is so much more than physical attraction. Confidence, manner of speech and movement, even something as elementary as body odor or pheromones affects a couple's ability to make love. Regardless of the type of intimacy or the degree of experimentation, the characters must always trust in their partner. Even if this is only on an instinctual level, when they are little more than strangers.

Every book is seen through the tinted glasses of the characters, and this includes sex. So which key factors do you have to take into account when scribbling down a sex scene?

One: Attraction

Attraction plays a key role. While we may not always be able to define it, the characters will. All characters have their own tastes— and to the hero and heroine, their chosen sex partners will embody that taste. That's not to exclude blemishes and imperfections—everyone has those—but these minor details, which might seem all-encompassing to the main character, will be details which her lover can easily overlook.

Sex is the physical demonstration of two people's attraction toward one another. It is not solely dependent on the way a person looks. The texture of her skin or hair, the way he smells or tastes, all of the senses come into play. These aspects need to be desirable or intriguing to the hero and heroine.

In my short erotic story *Cinnamon and Spice* the heroine Melissa believes that Jack is not her type. Does that mean there isn't attraction between them? Quite the opposite, in fact. While Melissa thought her "type" was macho, muscular men, after agreeing to a date with Jack she discovers that thin, sensitive computer nerds can be just as appealing. At the beginning of the book, two physical characteristics called to her despite trying to block them out. His earnest eyes—and his deep, shiver-inducing voice. Hard to say no when confronted by a voice made for whispering naughty things.

Whether or not your characters admit it, there must be a deep-seated attraction between them for the story to progress. Focus on what they find most desirable. What physical trait turns them on the most?

Two: Tension

Before the story can progress to sex, there needs to be some form of sexual tension. Why? Because the love scene, essentially, is the culmination of sexual anticipation. The absence of something makes the attainment that much sweeter. And I don't just mean for the characters. This tension is essential for the reader's benefit, too.

Just like a mystery novelist lines up red herrings, romance writers should sprinkle interactions with sexual tension. Scenes that seem like they might lead up to the big deed, but then are interrupted or one character backs off. The lingering desire is still there, but it lies unfulfilled.

This technique can be applied not only to full-length novels or novellas but also to short stories. *Cinnamon and Spice* is limited by length and features only one sex scene. But that scene is exalted by the tension crammed into the beginning. Despite Melissa's misgivings, Jack continues to weave his sensual tapestry around them both. Laying down unspoken promises with every word, every casual touch. At first, Melissa resists, but even those inner protests are eventually silenced.

How long should you keep up the tension? Picture an elastic band. You can stretch it and stretch it and stretch it— but eventually, it snaps. You don't want to bring the tension to the point that the reader would rather hurl the book (or worse, e-reader) at the wall rather than finish. There's a sweet spot, just before breaking. It sometimes takes finesse to reach. Ramp up the tension until your characters—and by extension, you—can't wait even another minute. This is the first step in bringing your characters to a mindless state.

Three: Emotion

Sex is not purely about the physical. It's about demeanor, anticipation, and the sensory. But most of all it's about emotion. Vulnerability, dependency, selfishness and selflessness all have their place.

Every sex scene in a romance novel should bare the characters. Completely. Not only are their bodies exposed but also their thoughts, their ambitions, and their feelings toward their partner. In most of my romances, the characters fall in lust before they fall in love. Why? Because emotion is tied into the act of sex. The characters learn things about each other, connect on a physical and metaphysical level, and essentially fall in love while distracted by their passion. It is for this reason that Seamus, in *Stone Cold Kiss*, felt comfortable enough with Kelsey after one intimate night with her to ask her to move to Ireland. This sort of emotional connection also helped to get Colleen, in *Never a Princess, Always a Frog*, out of her shell when confronted with a far more outrageous night than she expected.

How do you bring the emotion through? With little things. In order to draw out the full spectrum of the characters' feelings, you need to bring them to the edge. To a mindless state. Have them confront one of their fears. Maybe a character has trouble having orgasms without the aid of a vibrator or has never had a screaming orgasm, but comes swiftly at the hands of her lover. Maybe she craves pain but fears its application. Maybe he experiments with a new position or an array of sex toys.

In *Never a Princess, Always a Frog*. Colleen's scope of sexual experiences is a narrow one. In fact, she's stepping outside of her skin just by trying to attract a stranger for a one-night stand. Dan gives her that night of mind-blowing passion she's craved, and her first taste at being the recipient of oral sex. She can't get him out of her mind, but she's afraid he'll reject her in the morning light. From Dan's point of view, Colleen is the only woman who has interested him since his wife passed away. Giving her pleasure and new experiences invokes the primal, possessive part of him. She fills the empty hole he's been seeking to mend all along. So he's not so ready to let her go, either.

Whatever the case, the characters learn something new about themselves, something that ties them to their partner. This feeling of something new or raw, this impression of their partner is necessary for the relationship to continue. Because there is the necessary backslide—should the character continue to see this person? If one character thinks it's a mistake, the pursuant needs something concrete to convince him to continue the chase. Rakes and players need a reason to focus on the heroine exclusively. The first time they have sex is that reason.

Take *Stone Cold Kiss*, for example. After their first night together, Seamus feels comfortable enough to ask Kelsey to relocate. But Kelsey is a different matter altogether. Because of her convictions regarding relationships, she takes the first opportunity to skedaddle. She doesn't want to fall in love because she's sure it will lead to heartbreak—but Seamus is a persistent one, and takes it upon himself to continue to woo her even while they're oceans apart. He knows she's worth the trouble.

Showing vulnerabilities during sex is the first step toward the knowledge that the hero and heroine can't be apart. Great sex can bring their guards down and let them show their true thoughts and desires without worrying about the consequences. Through sex, they can open up to their partner without even realizing it.

Four: Sexual Confidence
So what makes for mind-boggling sex? Sexual confidence.

Both the hero and heroine must be comfortable enough in their skins to let the night progress as it will. This might not be the norm for them. Perhaps the heroine is uncomfortable with her physical appearance. Maybe she is a virgin or had a negative sexual experience. These things help to define the character and make her three-dimensional. But between the hero and the heroine, that awkwardness and uncertainty should melt away. Something about their partner should help the characters to overcome the doubt and anxiety plaguing them. It takes trust to have sex, doubly so if the characters are experiencing something new.

If plagued by insecurities, the heroine needs to be set at ease by her lover. Reassurances help. Or a picture painted with words, dirty talk about exactly what will happen in the next few minutes, in excruciating detail. Possibly even while enacting the scene. Humor is also a device which can be used if a character needs a little help relieving her fears. Whatever the means, in the end she will be left accepting. Open. Sometimes, as in *Never a Princess, Always a Frog*, these fears can be overcome with nothing more or less than all-consuming lust. While Colleen finds her body as physically attractive as a dried twig, Dan's insistent reaction to her teaches her to be a vixen in his arms. And from there, the night can begin.

Only when completely relaxed will the main characters have the courage to explore, to tease and be teased, to try new things. Romance is about pushing your characters' personal boundaries through interactions with each other and watching them grow as a result. Learning sexual confidence is key.

Five: Depth of Penetration

In the end, a sex scene is only as hot as will fit with the characters' natures. A conservative character probably won't have a threesome or anal sex. A dominant character will despise not being in control.

Forcing your characters to go against their natures won't work. Sometimes you won't even realize you're doing it. You'll be stuck, or your prose will be flat. It's hard at times, but don't think in terms of heat level. Just let your characters do as they will. In my own books, I have an array of heat levels. The heroine in *Unveiling His Princess* was uncomfortable with the thought of having sex before marriage. She may have gotten swept away with passion a time or two, but the consummation scene was left to the end. At the other end of the spectrum, the heroine in *Winter Worship* was bold enough not only to have sex with a stranger, but to do it in a public place.

Heat level is not only a matter of the sexual acts described in a scene, but also *how* they are described. A skilled writer will be able to make even vanilla sex all-consuming. So you don't need to worry about what your character will and will not do in bed—as long as you ramp up the description. If you can bring your character to a mindless state, you'll satisfy your reader as well. That alone will keep a reader coming back for more.

The Law of Attraction spurs on not only the natural world, but also the characters you create. Story thrives on diversity and conflict, but people build on what they know. Your characters have to be comfortable in their skin before they will be able to enact hot sex scenes. No one will go further than she's comfortable with—and a deep seated trust in the hero is essential. Trust must be based on something familiar, consciously or unconsciously so. And once the characters acknowledge and give into this tension—that's when the sparks start to fly. That's when the attraction will come alive off the page.

L.K. Below wants you to stay in touch!
Website: www.lbelow.net
Twitter: twitter.com/LBelowtheauthor
Facebook: http://on.fb.me/LKBelowFB
Goodreads: http://bit.ly/LKBelowGR
Email: lbelow@lbelow.net

7
WRITING THE FINE LINE BETWEEN EROTICA AND PORN
BY KATE DOUGLAS

About Kate Douglas:

Kate Douglas was the bestselling lead author for **Kensington's** erotic romance imprint, **Aphrodisia.** Her first book in the **Wolf Tales** series, which launched the new line in January 2006, led to twenty more novels and novellas in the series, and two other erotic paranormal series.

She's been published with Kensington, Ellora's Cave, Changeling Press, Beyond the Page Publishing, and is now with St. Martin's Press.

Known for her edgy, sexy stories skirting the boundaries of what is and isn't acceptable, Kate continues to push limits with her sensual Chanku shapeshifters in the Spirit Wild series. However, no matter how explicit the scenes, she maintains the lush, emotional aspect of the romance, keeping it paramount to each story.

Writing the Fine Line Between Erotica and Porn
by Kate Douglas

And a fine line it is. For those of us who write erotic romances, that niggling little question as to whether or not we've "crossed the line" often intrudes on our muse, especially when she's just guided us through a graphic love scene. You know the kind—the one where we realize we've managed to arouse not only our hero and heroine but ourselves as well.

Don't deny it—it happens to all of us if we're doing it right. Deep down inside we're thrilled to have written something so passionate, so filled with emotion and creative sexual technique that the scene takes on an intimate quality far beyond the romances our mothers used to read.

Well, we're not writing our mothers' romances. We're writing erotic romances, an entirely new breed of cat. The problem is, while we're busy breaking new ground in the publishing industry, we're also trying to define our own parameters.

Let's start with the definitions. ***Pornography*** — writings, pictures, etc. intended primarily to arouse sexual desire.

Okay...our stories often arouse sexual desire, yet we bristle when someone refers to them as porn. "No, they're erotic, not porn." Okay, so what's the definition of "erotic?"

Erotic—of or arousing sexual feelings or desires; having to do with sexual love; amatory.

Interesting...we just added two new words to the process: ***love*** and ***amatory***. We all know what love is, right? That brings us to yet another definition: ***Amatory***—of, causing, or showing love, especially sexual love.

Brings us right back to "love" again, something woefully lacking in pornography. So, we're writing "erotic **romance**." Indulge me. I'm on a roll, here...so I'll add the definition of romance. Be patient—it's a bit longer than the others:

Romance—a fictitious tale of wonderful and extraordinary events, characterized by a nonrealistic and idealizing use of the imagination; a type of novel in which the emphasis is on love, adventure, etc.; the type of literature comprising such stories; excitement, love, and adventure of the kind found in such literature; romantic quality or spirit; the tendency to derive great pleasure from romantic adventures; romantic sentiment; a love affair.

"Romance, adventure, excitement...a love affair." Has all the makings of a plot, doesn't it? Something else pornography generally lacks. Think of it this way—pornography is titillation for titillation's sake. It has few other redeeming qualities. There's lust without passion, sex without emotion or, to put it bluntly, screwing without the love. Tab A goes into slot B, C or maybe even D, everyone gets off, end of story.

Not in an erotic romance. Tabs may go into just as many slots, but there's a reason it happens. Motivation, strong characterization, a plot that draws the reader through the bedroom door with as much anticipation as the hero or heroine feels. Arousal comes from the connection an author establishes between her characters and her reader, a sense of knowledge and wonder strong enough to make the reader care what happens to the characters in the story, to make what happens between protagonists an intimate and meaningful experience.

It's a well known fact that a whole lot of any woman's sexual desire takes place between her ears. We are, by nature, cerebral beings with a sex drive that originates in the brain and eventually gets to the other erogenous zones. Just as it takes a skilled lover to bring a woman to orgasm, it takes a skilled writer to involve the reader in the sensuality of her characters' experience.

That means involving the emotions. We may have to listen to jokes about writing "one-handed reads," but I love the fact that the one hand that's busy, for many of my readers, is the one holding the hankie when something in my story moves her to tears.

You don't wring tears out of a reader with pornography.

You don't bring your reader to laughter, make them ache when the story takes a bad turn, send them looking for someone to hug when the plot grows so intense, with porn. You do it with an erotic romance that has so captured the reader's emotions, so completely involved all her senses that the experience becomes as intimate as life itself.

I'm certainly not against writing a sex scene that's hot, that's graphic, that turns my reader on and makes her run after a significant other or, when in need, something battery operated. I love getting email from readers who tell me they read "the hot stuff" to their husbands and love what it does for their marriages, and believe me, I've learned that, for an author of erotic romance, there's no such thing as an email with "TMI." I've heard it all and imagine I'll hear a lot more.

I do, however, like to think what makes my stories hot is the combination of plot, character, motivation—in essence, good writing. I like to think I manage to walk that fine line between pornography and romance without tipping over to the dark side, that my characters are powerful enough to take my graphic sex scenes beyond the single dimension of pornography and on into something stronger, better, more powerful.

It's not just sex. It's passion, emotion, arousal, love and desire. It's a character willing to give their life, to sacrifice whatever is important in order to be with the one he or she loves. It's a story that taps into every human emotion and leaves the reader laughing or crying, aroused or smiling or all of the above, but most of all, satisfied, and wondering what else the author has written.

As writers of erotic romance, we probably have a more intimate relationship with our fans than any authors in any other genre. We owe it to our readers to adhere carefully to that fine line separating our work from pornography, to remember the importance of good writing, strong stories and well-drawn characters.

We owe it to ourselves, as well. I want my writing legacy to be something I'm proud of, not something I'll look back on

with embarrassment or dismay. When in doubt, remember—
it's all about the romance.

Kate Douglas wants to stay in touch!
Website: katedouglas.com
Email: kate@katedouglas.com.
Facebook at www.facebook.com/katedouglas.authorpage
Follow her on Twitter: Twitter.com/wolftales
Subscribe to her newsletter at:
 KateDouglas-subscribe@yahoogroups.com

8
HOW TO WRITE CONVINCING FETISH AND NICHE MARKET SEX
BY GISELLE RENARDE

About Giselle Renarde:

Giselle Renarde is an All Romance Lesbian, Contemporary, and Interracial Category bestselling erotic fiction author. She's been published with Amber Quill Press, Cleis Press, Circlet Press, eXcessica Publishing, Hudson Audio Publishing, loveyoudivine Alterotica, New Dawning Bookfair, Ravenous Romance, Secret Cravings Publishing, Shadowfire Press, Torquere Press, Untreed Reads, and Xcite Books.

Reviewers are saying, "I love the erotic works of Giselle Renarde. She is a wonderful author with an instinctive flair for writing realistic characters to whom readers can easily relate," and, "if you want your romance with a strong story and a whole lot of sizzle, you must check out Giselle Renarde."

Giselle Renarde is a queer Canadian, avid volunteer, symphony groupie, theatergoer, and donut eater. She loves a gorgeous geek girl and lives across from a park with two bilingual cats who sleep on her head.

How to Write Convincing Fetish and Niche Market Sex
by Giselle Renarde

Girl meets boy, girl falls in love with boy, girl and boy have sex. In bed. With the lights off. Oh, and he's also a werewolf. AND a vampire! Is this your idea of erotic fiction? If so, that's cool. Mainstream erotic romance has huge appeal and a great following. But if you're into writing sex that might be a little quirky, a little kinky, or off the beaten path in some other way, this essay is for you.

There are all kinds of niche markets for erotica you might be interested in exploring, if you haven't already. BDSM erotica has already developed mass appeal, but that doesn't mean every author writing it has a deep understanding of the lifestyle. In this essay, I encourage readers to develop a firm understanding of their subject matter, particularly when writing erotica involving fetish, BDSM, and stories about gay, lesbian, bisexual, queer, and transgender characters.

What is fetish erotica, anyway? Is it the same as BDSM?

BDSM stands for Bondage, Domination (also Discipline), Submission (also Sadism) and Masochism. While there are certainly overlaps between BDSM and fetish erotica, these categories are not necessarily one and the same. BDSM can be executed without fetish, and fetish erotica can be written without so much as a hint in the direction of Domination and submission.

A fetish, the way I learned it back in university (I know—now you're asking, *like, what school did you go to*, right?) involves the displacement of one object by another. In a sexual sense, that translates to the displacement of the sexual organs by an object. The fetish object stands in place of the body to, in effect, de-familiarize it. In masking the body, the fetish itself becomes eroticized. An excellent example would be fishnet stockings—or any stockings, for that matter, but fishnets have become eroticized to such an extent they best illustrate my point:

Picture a foot slowly entering the stockings, and that material expanding as the foot, the ankle, the whole leg plunge deep inside, filling it right up. What act does this image conjure to mind? Putting on a pair of stockings is an innocuous activity until it's infused with the erotic. The fishnets become so symbolic of that which is desired that they, in effect, become the desire.

In erotica, fetish has acquired a much looser, less academic definition than the one I've provided above. Fetish has come to designate anything from which we derive enjoyment, beyond the body itself—could be opera gloves or hot wax or cross-dressing or raw ginger. A fetish object might have developed into a requirement for sexual arousal. Note that "Fetish" has become quite the umbrella term, so when it's used out there in the publishing world, it's used broadly and also conflated with the term "kink."

Like the fishnet example above, the following short excerpt from my lesbian fetish story *No Love, No Glove* (appears in *Sugar and Spice: A Collection of Kinky Girl-on-Girl Stories* from Ravenous Romance) briefly describes a clothing fetish:

***

Dragica's brow furrowed. She turned back to the computer before saying, "You can't just put on your damn gloves and expect me to jump into bed when I'm in the middle of something."

"Yes I can." That was the whole point—Nicky's butch babe couldn't resist her in a sleek pair of opera gloves. She picked up the long left-hand glove and rolled the stretchy fabric. When Dragica again offered no reaction, she slid her fingers and her thumb into the tight black holes. God, it felt good to get this slinky yet elegant material against her skin! She rolled the fabric up her forearm, past her elbow, and all the way to her bicep. She'd forgotten how sexy the gloves made her feel. No wonder Dragica couldn't resist her in them.

***

In fetish erotica, it is essential to showcase your characters' physical and psychological reactions to the fetish item. Your characters can fetishize anything at all, but I as a reader probably won't immediately relate to, say, a love of old dishtowels. If your chosen fetish object is particularly obscure in the erotic realm (or even if it isn't) it's crucial that we as readers be able to clearly understand through strong narrative, internal monologue, and dialogue why these old dishtowels are turning her on. We don't necessarily need the whole history of how she first became sexually aroused by kitchen linens (although that could be fun to hear about too), but we absolutely need to hear, in your character's voice, how that gingham print reminds her of romantic picnics, or how unforgiving the fabric feels against her skin when a partner ties her to the fridge.

In short, get your readers on board by describing your characters' physical and psychological reactions to the fetish object. In fetish erotica, there's no room to assume.

I don't really "get" BDSM. Is it okay to write about something I don't understand?

It's a very, very, very bad idea to write what you don't understand. You don't necessarily have to write within your realm of experience, but having a good understanding of the actions and interactions you're portraying is crucial in sculpting a convincing story. As Selena Kitt of eXcessica Publishing always says, "You don't have to be a murderer to write a murder mystery." Even so, submitting a story that displays how unacquainted you are with good practices of BDSM and the genre as a whole will not only cause the editor to scratch her head with one hand and send you a rejection letter with the other, it will very likely add you to that editor's mental list of uninformed authors they're not keen to work with.

Bryn Colvin, formerly the publisher of loveyoudivine Alterotica, has said on blog posts that she's read far too many unsolicited pseudo-BDSM stories. She's rejected them just as quickly because the authors of these works were clearly uninformed, misinformed, or otherwise ignorant of the concepts of true Domination and submission. "Between dealing with story submissions and personal reading, I've encountered some really awful material on the subject of submission, written by people who manifestly don't get it...I've read stories, from the perspective of the 'submissive' tracking this journey into non-existence. And really, they're horrible." Bryn goes on to say that "a lot of people do not know what the differences are between a Dom and a bully. Power exchange is about power, obviously, but it's also about trust." Remember: abuse, rape, or any character's subjection to non-consensual sex or violence does NOT fall into the category of BDSM. Submitting this type of fiction to an editor who, like Bryn, is interested in portrayals of Domination and submission, will not land you in that editor's good books.

If you want to try your hand at writing any given topic, particularly in niche market erotica such as fetish, BDSM, and even gay, lesbian, bisexual, and transgender fiction (often abbreviated to GLBT, or LGBTQ with Q standing for queer or questioning), make sure to do your homework first. In the long run, it's better to put in the time researching and feeling comfortable with a topic before you put pen to page—or, more likely, fingers to keyboard. Otherwise, you potentially face being blackballed by editors or, if your work is picked up, poor reviews and future "What was I thinking?" woes. Save yourself those future headaches and do the research now.

What constitutes research? Often, that depends on your comfort level in terms of interacting with people in new situations. Some authors go to play parties and dungeons to research their next BDSM book. Other authors say, "I write to minimize my interactions with other people. That's way out of my comfort zone!" That's fine, too. If you're not comfortable attending an event or talking with people who live that lifestyle face to face, just make sure you put in some solid online research hours.

Where do I look online for reliable information?

Good question. The last thing you want to do is read one and only one BDSM story online and base your entire approach on that. Just think: the author of that story might have had absolutely no idea what they were writing about! To find out what appeals to kinksters, go where the kinsters are. Websites like FetLife or Kink Academy will allow you to observe a broad range of kinksters in action, and you might even get up the nerve to ask a few people about their proclivities. Just make sure not to ask any questions in a manner that could be perceived as intrusive or judgmental. You'll end up getting cyber-slapped—and not in a good way!

I understand BDSM pretty well already, but sometimes I get stuck when I'm trying to think up kinky angles for a new story. How can I get past my BDSM writer's block?

When I want to get away from the same old ho-hum approach, I do a little shopping. Well, I don't usually buy anything, but I find that perusing a good BDSM gear/sex toy shop online gives me great ideas. Look through the items at a website like Stockroom and see what's available, what materials are out there, and what these toys or bondage equipment look like. If you need the sensual experience of seeing, touching, and even smelling an item, check out a bricks and mortar shop that sells this type of gear. Have you ever written a story about a cock cage? Puppy play? Bondage mitts? There are sub-niche markets for all sorts of things you may not even have fathomed. Learn the gear, understand the appeal, and allow the objects to bring out the D/s (Domination/submission) dynamic between characters.

Another angle, which might sound clichéd but really does work, is to look around your house with an eye to repurposing items for sexual use. My story *Dry Rub*, which appears in *Best Bondage Erotica 2012* (Cleis Press), involves a woman tying her husband's wrists to chrome dining chairs with two cloth dinner napkins. A husband spanks his adulterous wife with a wooden spoon in my story *Black Lace and Wood* (appears in *Six of the Best*

Spanking Stories from Xcite Books), and in my novella *Stacy's Dad Has Got It Going On* (eXcessica Publishing), an older man "tortures" his daughter's college roommate with ice cubes.

You can get as kinky as your imagination will let you with household objects. Purchasing sex toys and fetish gear is fun, but it gets pricey. Stories that involve objects most people have lying around their houses can spark a reader into action. Another more extreme example would be Pasha and Melanie's reuse of a water bottle to give Kathryn an enema in my kinky lesbian threesome e-book *Elementary, My Dear Kathryn*. The following excerpt from this anal fetish story also conveys some of Melanie's feelings about living as Pasha's submissive:

***

"She is going to leave that dress on," Pasha instructed.

Melanie offered a subtle nod and entered the bathroom. It was wonderfully large and sparkling white, in true hotel fashion. Pasha had pulled back the shower curtain. Her water bottle rested on the clean marble counter. It was full now, with warm water most probably, and the nozzle-lid was back on top. Pasha handed it to Melanie while Kathryn stood in the threshold. It was indeed warm. Not hot, but warm.

"Come inside," Melanie said. She never knew how she knew what Pasha desired. The expectations were inside of her. For Melanie, being a true submissive meant anticipating Pasha's needs and wishes, and acting on them without direction.

Tonight Melanie would clean Kathryn out and eat her ass. All for Pasha.

Kathryn took a single step into the bathroom, and then paused. Her gaze betrayed nothing. She didn't even seem confused. Could she possibly know what was coming? She seemed so innocent.

Watching the water bottle, Kathryn asked, "What should I do now?"

***

Remember, people have all kinds of different relationships, and those who share D/s lives are no exception. Even if you decide to use some unusual household item for inspiration, if your characters lack dimension your story might not bob to the surface of an editor's picks. Readers want more, which means editors are looking for stories that really pop. Give them something to remember.

I want to write about LGBTQ characters, but I don't know any queer people. Can I still write about them?

Because I write a great deal of fiction involving transgender and genderqueer characters, readers and aspiring authors often contact me with this question. In response, I tell them a story my twelfth grade English teacher once told me about the author W.P. Kinsella. He wrote a whole bunch of short stories that were set on First Nations Reserves in Canada. Those stories turned into a TV show called "The Rez" and received great critical acclaim. More than that, First Nations Peoples who read his work said, "Yes! This is my life on a page." They could really relate. So much so that they didn't believe Kinsella had never set foot on a Reserve in his life. He managed to convey the tenor and tone of "Rez" life convincingly. It can be done.

However...it can also be done badly. Very, very, very badly, judging by some of representations I've seen of transgender people, in particular. Keep in mind at all times that what you write matters. As an erotica writer, you probably hear the exact opposite message from friends and family—that what you write is inconsequential—but trust me when I say they are wrong. What you do is important on so many levels and will impact readers in ways you can't imagine. That's why it is vitally important to include accurate and responsible representations of LGBTQ characters, and characters of all ethnicities.

My authorial niche is transgender erotica. I started writing it because my significant other is transgender and we have many transgender friends. Because I was already an erotic fiction writer before we met, a complaint that often arose was that there was nothing out there depicting transgender people in a respectful and realistic light. There was a lot of "tranny/shemale" porn floating around, but nobody I knew had ever read a story they felt portrayed them accurately or kindly, as real human beings in loving and committed relationships.

"If everything you knew about trans people came from erotica, you'd think we were all freaks and drag queens and prostitutes," one friend said. What was lacking on the market was erotic romance involving transgender characters. So that's what I started to write: erotic fiction that portrayed transgender people as whole individuals, with real personalities, with body issues, with fears and aspirations. And when that work started getting published, word caught on fast among trans people that I was writing erotica that wasn't just *about* them, but that was actually *for* them!

The first story in my anthology *My Mistress' Thighs: Erotic Transgender Fiction and Poetry* is a piece of historical fiction. *The Public Life of Private Paulsen* is a love story between Pearl, one of the first trans women to undergo a "sex change operation," and George, the soldier she fought beside during the Second World War, back when Pearl was still known as Howard.

***

"This feels right, doesn't it Georgie?" Her words were quiet but racing. She didn't wait for a response before saying, "It feels right to me. It feels like this is the way we should have met to begin with, but the fact that we knew each other before…why, I think it gives you a more profound respect for me as a person."

George agreed wholeheartedly and told her so by easing her face up from his shoulder. When he felt her breath on his lips, he kissed her gently. That one slow kiss tasted so indescribably delicious it would have satiated his appetites if he hadn't already been naked. His cock pummelled Pearl's thigh, splashing it with liquids. She laughed, leading him toward the bed before tossing back the covers. When he was in beside her, she covered up their nudity and traced her hands the length of his flesh.

"My body," she told him, "it isn't like other girls'. Well, you knew that already. What I mean to say is that..." Reaching across his chest, she pulled open the bedside table's Bible drawer. He listened while she unscrewed the lid from a pot of something or other. "We'll need to use some jelly."

***

In queer fiction, as in all fiction, your characters are of the utmost importance. If the author doesn't empathize and respect them, their stories will not ring true. The proof is in the pudding: if you understand queer people, it will be evident in your work. When you write for a niche, write well and with sensitivity and knowledge, that market will seek you out. Lots of people are writing m/f (male/female) or even m/m (male/male) erotic romance. If you break the mold, you can acquire a devoted following. The major task is to get to the heart of your characters. Understand their background and how it formed them and continues to shape their actions and interactions.

But isn't erotica just fantasy anyway? Do my characters in queer and BDSM fiction really have to be relatable?

In one word? Yes. In more than one word, if your characters are not emotionally engaging and believable representations—whether they're gay, straight, vanilla, kinky, whatever—readers won't care about them. A reader who is not engaged with your characters on an emotional or even primitive level will not be interested in sticking around for the sex. Also, as a writer of trans fiction with strong ties to that community, I want to hit home the point that portraying transgender people as nothing but cardboard cut-out sluts, whores, and drag queens is really offensive—and most trans erotica does exactly that.

This is where we come to the difference between fetishizing *objects* and fetishizing *people*. When you write a piece that fetishizes a certain type of people (a Transgender fetish, Japanese Schoolgirl fetish, Big Black Guy fetish, etc) what you're ultimately doing is reinforcing stereotypes, and for the most part negative stereotypes, about people of certain ethnicities, sexual orientations, or gender identities. At all times, strive to put character first. The highest goal in writing fetish erotica is to create a piece that will appeal to and arouse even a reader who has never shared the fetish you're writing about, or never considered it before. That has to come out through your characters.

How do I know if I'm representing queer characters responsibly? I'm just writing the story as it comes to me. Are you saying I should self-censor?

There are a lot of things most publishers won't touch, and I'm seeing "negative or positive stereotyping" showing up more and more. At the same time, at least as far as m/m romance is concerned, I'm also seeing conversations about how inaccurately gay men are being portrayed as authors endeavor to write about "manly men" who are gay. So what's the solution? Again, I think it's to get deep inside your characters' hearts and know them inside out. If they come across as full and rounded people, with flaws and strengths and fears and hopes, they will be more than stereotypes.

That said, one theme that I see over and over again, which I find unappealing in the extreme, involves representing queer and bisexual characters as being orientated toward a same-sex partner only because there isn't a suitable opposite-sex partner available at the time. For instance, I've read too many books to list wherein a woman is attracted to another woman, a lesbian romance ensues, but then the "happy ever after" at the end of the book involves one or both of those women riding off into the sunset with a suitable *man*. I'm talking about books where we follow a lesbian love affair through its journey, and then we as readers are supposed to be happy that one or both of these lovers gets to settle down with a nice guy and lead a "normal" life.

As a queer woman, I find this kind of blatant reinforcement of heteronormativity in plot structure highly offensive, and my advice is to please stay away from it. My guess is that authors who are writing these plots have no idea their take on the "happily ever after" formula is so insulting to queer readers, but that's the whole point: the last thing you want in a niche market is for a reader to pick up your book and say, "You're writing about a character just like me, but you got it all wrong!"

Now, all this is not to say these "plotlines" don't occur in real life. Remember how up-in-arms many lesbians were when bisexual feminist singer/songwriter Ani DiFranco married a man? That wasn't fiction, that was real life, and it still angered many fans. Again, as will all stories, the motivation must come clearly through your characters. We as readers need to feel that this, whatever "this" happens to be, is the right decision for the character, or at least understand why she felt compelled in that direction.

Wow! There are so many pitfalls to writing for a niche market. Now that I know how to avoid them, how do I get it right?

Build believable characters, first and foremost. When writing fetish erotica, focus on sensation, the relation of object to sensation, and the impact a fetish object has on your character's state of arousal. In many ways, vanilla erotica is easier because the sensations described are immediate and recognizable. If you write *he licked my pussy*, a reader will more than likely respond by thinking, "Oh, I know what that's like— it's good!" With acts that are not as highly relatable, or which are definite kinks, the author has to work a little harder. We have to spell it out for the reader. It's not just *this feels good*, but *why does it feel good?* Does it generate in your character a feeling of power, of humiliation, of femininity? What feeling do they crave and how does the object satisfy it?

Writing sex for a niche market is definitely not straightforward as writing vanilla erotica. It's less relatable to general readers, so you have to spell it out for them, and seasoned kinksters want to be sure you know your stuff, so you have to spell it out for them as well. A solid psychosexual bearing is required, but the payoff, in terms of customer loyalty and word of mouth as well as respect and gratitude from a given community is huge. My most heart-warming reader comments have all been in relation to my niche market sex. These readers saw themselves in the characters I'd written, and as a result, the sex those characters shared resonated tremendously.

Keep this advice in mind as you write, and you're sure to conquer the fetish and niche market.

Giselle Renarde wants you to stay in touch!
Website: www.wix.com/gisellerenarde/erotica
Blog: donutsdesires.blogspot.com
Email: gisellerenarde@yahoo.com
Twitter: twitter.com/GiselleRenarde
Goodreads: goodreads.com/gisellerenarde

9
SEXY SENTENCES
BY CHARLOTTE STEIN

About Charlotte Stein:

Charlotte Stein is an Amazon best-selling erotic romance author. She's been published with HarperCollins Mischief, Avon Impulse, Random House/Black Lace, Ellora's Cave, Xcite, Cleis Press, Total-E-Bound, and Constable and Robinson.

Recently she was a finalist in the annual Dear Author and Smart Bitches competition DABWAHA with her book *Run To You*.

She likes midget gems, watching terrible sitcoms and being psycho-analyzed by sexy, super traumatized FBI agents.

Sexy Sentences
by Charlotte Stein

I guess everyone, at some point, has asked themselves what makes a sex scene sexy. Or at least, everyone who likes reading sexy stories has. Most of the other people who don't dare to read the Devil's Words are probably just asking themselves about their life choices, while crying.

But I digress. When what I really wanted to get into is what makes a sex scene sexy— which is a bit of a broad thing to look at. I mean, a lot of elements contribute to making a sexy sex scene. You need a good hero, of course. No point starting with some cross between a gorilla and that pimply guy from the video store. You're just heading for disaster, there, even if you give this unholy hybrid the personality of a God.

So now that we've got my extensive theories on hot heroes all stowed away, let's tick the other boxes. You need a sexy setting (in a port-a-potty coated in shit is probably a bad idea), a sexy scenario (you won't get much tension out of "let's maybe have sex in between cutting my toenails and getting the kids up"), and a willingness to go to sexy places (if you're afraid of saying the word *bottom*, you're probably in the wrong career).

And once you've gotten all of these things and arranged everyone's body parts and made sure you haven't had someone take their bra off twice, you can finally get to the main area in which I think so many writers fall down.

Because to me, there is nothing less sexy than having all these things in place: amazing set-up, great setting, lots of tension, great, hot characters…and then letting them all down with banal, repetitive or poor sentence structure.

The latter is an obvious one, I feel. Poor sentence structure will let any story down. You don't want seventeen commas jammed into one line about your hero's cock—anyone knows that. I mean, just picture it:

"She ran, a hand, down over, his immense, glistening, shaft."

No no no no what? What? Don't do that. Don't even do

half of that. And don't do the opposite of that, either, because that's just as annoying:

"She ran a hand down over his immense glistening shaft while he put a hand in her hair and kissed her lips because he loved her."

Ugh, no. I'm talking about glistening shafts, here, and yet somehow the sexiness is just dead. It has been killed. And all for the want of more or less punctuation!

However, I feel the above is somewhat obvious. If you're here and reading this, chances are you know not to forget the comma exists, or conversely—fall in love and marry it. And really, mastering the basics of punctuation is the easiest thing any writer has to do, whether you're writing sexy scenes or not.

But when we get into the area of "banal, repetitive sentence structure", things get a little stickier. Because technically, there's nothing wrong with sentences like this: "He took out his cock and showed her it. Then he rubbed her shoulder and kissed her. It was then he knew the depth of his arousal."

But it simply doesn't work. It can't even be called mildly interesting, never mind sexy and arousing. There's just something so mechanical about it, like a mildly erotic set of stereo instructions.

"Take pole A. Insert into socket B. Adjust insertion point until desired level of reception occurs."

I mean, come on. No one wants to read that. They want to read a bit of variety, and see a bit of energy in sexy writing—all of which can be achieved by the simple introduction of a few commas, a few different sentence lengths, a few "ands" here and a few simple sentences/fragments there. *Et voila*:

***

He slowly peeled his jeans down his legs, revealing little glimpses of the curve of his ass, the muscles in his thighs, and finally the perfect length of his cock. She wanted to reach for him immediately but he stopped her. Kissed her. Rubbed her shoulder in a way that made her go weak all over. It seemed clear how much he wanted this, but she couldn't say for sure until he pushed her back on the bed.

At which point, the real games began.

***

Hopefully you get the gist, which is mainly about sentence variation but also about how you achieve this—*by spreading the action out.*

Now don't get me wrong. Action is great. Actual action is the backbone of a good sexy story. There's nothing worse than erotica that avoids all the best stuff in favour of fancy thoughts about nothing, or dialogue that focuses on what the main characters had for dinner.

But action has to be balanced with other stuff, or else you get that repetitive, where-do-I-put- this-wire effect. Ignoring the thoughts, feelings, speaking bits etc, of your characters actually leaves you with those bare bones sentences, and it strips the sexy right out of your story.

Because readers want the whole experience. They want to know how things taste, touch, feel, sound and look. They want to know through actions, through inner monologue, and through actual spoken words. Ignore any of this, and you leave your story short.

So now that I've talked a bit about the issue of sentence length and how you can stop those dreaded series of stereo instructions, I just wanted to briefly touch on the starts of sentences and how that can cause problems, too.

Because combining a lack of variety in sentence length/structure with the same beginning over and over—to me, that's just the worst. It's just the worst of the worst. It kills a scene dead, in my opinion, when you get something like this:

"She kissed him when he asked her to. She leant forward, and put her lips on his. She didn't know if he wanted it hard or fast. She did it anyway."

And all right, that's a bit of an extreme example. But hopefully you can see the effect that overuse of a word at a start of a sentence has. Even if you've got the varied sentences, using the word "she" or the word "he" at the start of a sentence again and again is jarring—in much the same way that overuse of any word is.

Of course, you can usually get away with using a lot of little words—people will notice if you use "exponentially" twice in one paragraph, but they won't notice if you use "it's". However, the threshold of word overuse is exponentially (tee hee) increased when said word is at the start of a sentence. Suddenly, it becomes glaring.

And, in my opinion, un-erotic. Because really, anything that pulls you out of the seamless erotic action—even something as slight as word repetition that isn't a stylistic choice—can kill the mood that's been set up.

For example:

"She loved the way he touched her. She couldn't believe how good it felt, how right. She had to touch him in return, and let him know that she enjoyed everything he did. She stroked his cheek, then his arm, then lower and lower until..."

Is far less sexy (to me, at least) than something like this:

"She loved the way he touched her. It felt so good, so right, and she simply had to touch him return. He needed to know that she enjoyed everything he did, even if she could only tell him through a stroke over his cheek, or a caress of his arm, or hint that she wanted to go lower, lower..."

And if you don't find the latter sexier, well, that's cool. Get down with your awesome self. You've probably mastered the ability to use lots of short sentences with the same start without sounding like you've written a cookbook. .

But personally, I can't do it. And when I encounter it in otherwise amazing sexy stories, it does pull me out of the scene.

So does a complete lack of deep point of view (POV).

Now, if you regularly avoid all of the stuff I've just talked about, you're probably already getting pretty deep into the point of view of your characters. Varied sentence length, structure and beginnings go hand in hand with this whole deep POV thing, for reasons too complicated for me to understand.

Though I'm going to attempt to explain it anyway—

basically, deep POV is all about getting under your character's skin, whereas constantly starting a million short sentences with the word "she" distances you from the character automatically. Putting the word "she" in there immediately suggests that you are the author and you are controlling your character, and though there's nothing wrong with that in decently sized doses, too much of it puts your character on Earth and the reader on Mars.

That's the level of distance we're talking here.

Deep POV is all about starting inside the character. Which is totally not a pun even in all the parts where it is. Basically, instead of going with this:

"She ate the spaghetti. She thought it tasted delicious."

Try this:

"God, the spaghetti looked good. Before he'd even turned around, she'd wolfed down half the plate."

Which is a pretty basic example, but hopefully illustrates what I'm trying to say: start *inside* the action. Don't let shit get in the way. Don't be afraid to put in little direct snippets of your character's thoughts, like this:

"Fuck – he knew already."

Instead of this:

"Fuck, she thought. He knew already."

It just gives a scene more immediacy, more intimacy—something that's vital for good erotic writing.

Which is not to say that you should start overloading your writing with lots of Gods and fucks. Or that you need tons of deep POV all of the time, loads of non-short sentences and no use of the word "she".

I think the best thing, as always, is to use a bit of everything in moderation. Keep an eye on repetition, watch out for a lack of variety—these things have helped me, I believe, and I think they're useful for any writer.

Now go forth and write and some sexy sentences!

Charlotte Stein wants you to stay in touch!
Website: charlottestein.net
Twitter: twitter.com/charlotte_stein
Goodreads: goodreads.com/charlottestein
Email: charlotte_stein@hotmail.co.uk

10
FIGHTING SEX
BY ISABO KELLY

About Isabo Kelly:

Isabo Kelly is an award-winning, multi-published erotic romance author. She's currently published with Samhain Publishing, Ellora's Cave, Tirgearr Publishing, Cerridwen Press/Blush, Crescent Moon Press, and Ravenous Romance, has been published with Echelon Press, Zumaya Publishing, LTD Books and Dreams Unlimited, and had a short story published in Romantic Times Magazine.

Reviewers have called Isabo's books "Hot, hot, hot…", "sexy, fun…", "fast-paced, page turning…" and "Beautifully romantic…Isabo Kelly is one author you should add to your auto buy list."

Isabo's gypsy soul has taken her around the world, including many years living in Ireland where she got her Ph.D. in animal behavior. She's worked with all sorts of animals including sharks, snakes, lizards, and dolphins. Now she's a stay-at-home mom and a full-time writer, living in New York City with her brilliant Irish husband, her two sons and their mad dog.

Fighting Sex
by Isabo Kelly

Intense, action-packed, emotional, potentially dangerous, and reveals a lot about who and what your characters are. What type of scene does that describe? If you guessed a fight scene and a sex scene, you'd be right.

In fact, these two scenes have more in common than many people might realize. And you can learn a lot about writing a good sex scene by studying the way fight scenes are written. When done well, both add levels of intensity and emotion to a story. But these scenes have to matter each and every time. They have to add to the plot and to character development. And that's the trick with writing erotic romance, to manage so much sex without it getting boring.

So what do both fights and sex have in common? Each of these scenes has four major elements that are necessary to both to make them important and engaging for readers: emotion, choreography, believability, and character. Let's look at these characteristics in a little detail.

Emotion

Emotion is what distinguishes erotica and erotic romance from porn. Emotion is what makes each scene significant to the plot and the characters. And you can't write either a convincing fight scene or a convincingly erotic sex scene without this element.

What emotions are portrayed depends on your characters and what you want from the scene. Even the most jaded protagonist will get a charge from being in a fight or from having sex. There is always some kind of emotion involved, even if that emotion is not what a reader might expect.

This fight scene is from my fantasy romance, THE HERON'S CALL, published with Samhain Publishing. In this scene, the warrior heroine, Rowena, has just flashed back to a traumatic afternoon many years earlier and it's put her on an emotional edge. She turns her fear and pain into a fight with the hero.

***

Gods, he'd probably seen her tears. Humiliated, she started back to camp, but he stopped her with a hand on her shoulder. She spun around to face him and without thinking, her sword was in her hands. "Leave me alone, Kael. I mean it."

"No. Tell me what's wrong. Why are you crying?"

"I'm not. And it's none of your business anyway."

His eyes narrowed, sparked with a dangerous glimmer. "Yes. It is." He pulled his own sword from the sheath strapped over his back, touched his blade to hers. "Winner take all," he murmured.

"You don't want to fight me."

"You're right. I want to fuck you. You're the one insisting on a fight. So we'll play your way first. Then we play mine."

Her fear morphed to anger. "Arrogant bastard." She spun away then swung back to catch his blade with her own, the sound of steel on steel ringing in the dark copse. There wasn't a lot of room between the trees, but she used what she had, unleashing her anger and frustration, slashing, testing, pushing him to show her just how good he was.

He tried to back her against another tree, but she turned the trick on him, had him braced between bulging roots, barely able to deflect her attack as he untangled himself. She laughed at his growl, let the energy rushing through her wash away everything but the battle. Her muscles bunched and flexed, her feet danced, her blood pumped in time to the rhythm of the fight. "You underestimate me, Heron," she said, swinging her blade to push aside his blow.

"Never."

But on his next attack, he overstretched. She twisted around behind him and slapped him across the ass with the flat of her blade. She laughed, pleased with his yelp. As he turned on her, she continued to grin, enjoying herself, reveling in the play of skill against skill. He was good. Very good. And it made the battle more exciting.

***

Notice it's not so much the fight itself but the way the two characters are reacting and how they feel that matters here. Rowena enjoys a good fight and losing herself in this one lets her forget her fear. Contrary to what a reader might expect a character to feel, Rowena is using this particular duel to bury feelings of hurt and confusion so she doesn't have to deal with them. And it's those conflicting emotions that make this fight scene important to the story.

Choreography

That example also demonstrates the importance of choreography. Not only is this an important element in a fight scene, it's vital in a sex scene. There is nothing more disconcerting than having a heroine swing three different fists at a bad guy, and there's nothing quite so disturbing as having a hero manage to touch very different parts of the heroine's body with the same hand at the same time. If you're writing ménage or more stories, choreography is even more important. You have to keep track of all those various body parts to make sure no one has more than they're supposed to or are doing things that aren't possible. Remember where the various hands and feet are, make sure in edits that there are no extra breasts or penises involved (two breasts only for human women; one penis for human men—if you're writing about otherworldly creatures with more of these body parts, well, do keep in mind how many they have).

Maintaining that Suspension of Disbelief

Beyond just simple choreography, the movements through both sex and fight scenes have to be realistic—readers have to believe these movements are achievable. Yes, you might have paranormally endowed characters able to do things a normal human can't. But they still have to perform in ways that *seem* physically possible to the reader.

71

If you're not entirely sure if a position or set of movements is possible, consult books. There are dozens of martial arts and combat books that can walk you through a believable fight scene and convey how various weaponry can realistically be used. For sex, the Kama Sutra is an excellent resource. It not only outlines various sexual positions, it will tell you how fit you need to be to manage those positions. It also tells which are possible with various size combinations for men and women. If you're writing erotic romance, and you've followed the bandwagon and given your hero an enormous penis, there are certain positions that just will not work with a woman who happens to be small. If a reader clenches her knees together in sympathetic *pain* during a sex scene, the scene probably isn't very romantic or erotic for that matter.

For both choreography and believability, I also recommend watching movies (yes, this is giving you permission to watch porn if you can tolerate the tedium). Getting a good visual feel for what works and what doesn't will help inform your writing. Bear in mind, a lot of martial arts films are more…fantastical in their portrayal of battles. There are generally wires and harnesses involved. But, even using wires, the human body can only do what it can do. And knowing how far you can push your readers' sense of the possible will help immensely when crafting these scenes.

Here's an example where choreography and physical believability plays an important role in a sex scene. This is from my short paranormal romance story, *Mate Run*, in the FANG BANGERS anthology from Ravenous Romance.

***

A moment later, Max was on the branch too, near the trunk, once again in human form. She let her gaze travel across his golden skin, over the tightening muscles of his abdomen to the thick length of his erection. Licking her human lips this time, she rose on hands and knees and crawled toward him, balancing effortlessly on the thick limb. He reached back to hold the large trunk, a move that thrust his cock toward her.

She smiled and rose before him, taking his hard thickness into her mouth.

He didn't touch her, which was her preference, as she licked and sucked the length of his cock, swirling her tongue around the head and dipping the tip just beneath his foreskin. She heard the bark crunch under his grip and growled in pleasure. Even the precariousness of their position in the tree turned her on. And he knew it.

***

Since these are both paranormal characters (shape-shifting were-tigers), they obviously have good balance. But their position in a tree still has to be believable, and what they do up there has to be realistic for sex on a branch. Notice the characters are also aware of their precarious position. It's part of the thrill of this particular moment for them. And that awareness of the dangers adds to the believability of this choreography.

Character

While used for specific purpose, both of the previous examples manage to demonstrate each of the three necessary elements to good sex and good fights that have been discussed so far.

They also demonstrate the final, most important aspect of writing good sex and fight scenes. Character. Character is what distinguishes one scene from another. It's what makes them interesting, unique and pertinent to the story. How someone fucks and how they fight reveals more about them than even the character might realize. Sex and battle leave a person vulnerable. How they react to that vulnerability speaks to who they are as people, what they've been through, and how they are affected by the scene.

Are they changed? Have they gone somewhere they never thought they would, or is this just the kind of place they've always wanted to be? Are they angry, hollow, excited, in love, desperate, scared, bored? How they experience the events of the scene is much more important than what they do—especially in character-driven books like romances.

The following sex scene comes in the middle of my fantasy romance, BRIGHTARROW BURNING (from Samhain Publishing), after the hero and heroine have just escaped death.

***

[Layla's] body shook against the need. Too much. And not enough. The sense of being overwhelmed, the almost painful brush against her sensitive nerves, became welcome. Needed. She felt him everywhere. His hand moving along her spine made her arch. He squeezed her ass with his other hand and she rubbed against his erection, desperation riding her hard. She needed relief and she wasn't sure where to turn. To get away. To get closer.

Ulric took the debate out of her hands. He worked the lacings of her trousers loose and pushed the soft leather down her hips until they pooled around her ankles. Her feet were trapped, but that didn't stop him. He lifted her and she braced her thighs against his hips even as her feet stayed linked near his knees. She glanced down to see he'd already freed his erection from the confines of his own trousers and the sight of his straining cock made her overheated blood erupt.

Holding her around the waist with one hand, he moved her hips forward, positioning her so his tip nudged her opening. Liquid seeped down her thighs. The feel of him was a tease that only heightened her passion. She had a moment to be impressed by his strength—he held her entire weight without bracing against anything—then he pulled her hips down, ramming into her. And Layla screamed. He felt so good and thick and so damned right.

She let him take control of the rhythm because she could barely focus beyond the friction of his cock pumping into her and the bump of her swollen clit against him. Her orgasm rose quickly, painfully, and her body started to move of its own accord to reach that exquisite peak. With her shins braced against the tops of his knees, she had enough leverage to follow his movements and meet him stroke for pounding stroke.

He murmured her name against her neck, the warmth of his breath washing another wave of heat over her skin. And when his hands tightened on her waist and ass, her body finally broke. She came with another scream, a sound Ulric swallowed in a kiss. A moment later, she tasted his own groan as his every muscle stiffened. She clenched at his shoulders, holding him until she felt him relax again. Then she pulled back from their kiss to look him in the eyes.

What she saw there devastated her. Tenderness and fear all swirling together with a look of wonder. Did she look that way? She felt those same emotions. Could he see it in her eyes too? Did he know she loved him?

And was she just seeing what she wanted to see?

***

Again, we have the necessary choreography and a physically possible position that make the scene believable. We have a high level of emotional charge. Layla's been trying to resist Ulric, despite the fact that she loves him. Her near-death followed by their passionate sex left her emotions completely exposed to him. And that's what makes this sex scene different from all the others in the book. The sex itself is a reaction to a feeling of vulnerability and relief, but it opens Layla up to both Ulric and the reader. Both her character and his come through in ways that neither can convey in mere conversation. That revelation is what makes this scene important.

Nothing will turn an erotic romance reader off more than sex scene after sex scene that doesn't *mean* anything to the story. They might be reading erotic romances for the high sexual content, but they want story with their sex (even if the sex *is* the story). That's the difference between erotica and porn, between an action-packed battle scene and a pointless succession of bloody fights—character. It's all about the character.

If you want your erotica to sizzle, remember to fill your

scenes with emotion, choreograph them and make sure the movements of the characters are physically possible, and don't forget to make each and every scene do more than just show sex. If you're writing sex because you need to add more, or throwing in a fight to fill in space, don't. Your readers will put the book down.

And there's nothing worse than a reader setting aside an erotic book because they're bored with the sex!

Isabo Kelly wants you to stay in touch!
Website: IsaboKelly.com
Blog: IsaboRambles.blogspot.com
Email: isabokelly@verizon.net
Twitter: Twitter.com/IsaboKelly
Facebook: facebook.com/IsaboKelly
Goodreads:
   goodreads.com/author/list/722664.Isabo_Kelly

11
SO YOU THINK YOU CAN KINK?
BY DELPHINE DRYDEN

About Delphine Dryden:

Delphine Dryden writes contemporary erotic romance for Carina Press, and mainstream steampunk romance for Berkley Publishing. Her writing has earned an Award of Excellence and Reviewers' Choice Award from Romantic Times Book Reviews, an EPIC Award, and a Colorado Romance Writers' Award of Excellence. She's also a regular contributor to the group blog Wonkomance.com.

Reviewers have called Delphine's erotic romance "smoking hot quirky contemporary romance," "heartwarming and heartbreaking" books with "very sensual characters that you'll love getting to know". In a starred review of her second steampunk romance, Publishers Weekly said, "this romantic adventure shines, thanks to memorable characters, nifty steampunk technology, and undeniable chemistry between the leads."

Delphine writes full time and edits part time. She and her family are all Texas natives, and reside in unapologetic suburban bliss near Houston.

So You Think You Can Kink?
by Delphine Dryden

When I started writing erotic romance, I didn't set out to write BDSM. I was actually surprised when my second novel, When in Rio, was categorized as a BDSM romance. Sure, it had some spanking. Some bondage, a lot of Domination and submission, a bit of light paddling, and a whole lot of orgasm denial...but BDSM? I was just writing what I knew, frankly, and my own tastes have never run to the "typical" club-centered fantasy-style BDSM that I'd read—and disliked—in so many erotic novels. My tastes just run to spanking...and bondage, and Domination and submission, and...*oh.*

Normally I don't lead off writing discussions by talking about my sex life, but I think it's important to point this out because I see a lot of erotica writers trying to incorporate kink when it's clear they have no personal experience with the stuff, and sometimes it really shows. While I'm not in the crowd that feels you should only write BDSM if you've done it yourself, I do feel a certain amount of extra research and thought is vital if you're planning to write a BDSM erotic romance. Your readers deserve it, and it's a great chance to broaden your writing horizons.

We all write things without having experienced them directly, that's part of writing fiction. But when you're writing erotic romance scenes incorporating BDSM—whether you're an aficionado yourself or not—it's important to keep in mind why you're including the kink, what exactly the kink looks and feels like to your participants from a physical and mental standpoint, and what emotions are likely to arise before, during and after the kink interaction.

A very brief glossary:
Before going any further, here are a few terms you might find useful while reading this essay and while researching kink for your own writing (I've kept these as minimal as possible;

please be aware this is only a starting place, and these definitions are not meant to be definitive or exhaustive):

<u>BDSM</u>: Bondage, Domination, Submission, Masochism…or, depending on what your focus is, Bondage, Discipline, Sadism, Masochism. I will use this term pretty much interchangeably with "kink".

<u>Bottom</u>: the person on the receiving end of an interaction (this is a very, very brief way to explain this, and doesn't attempt to touch on the complexity of topping/bottoming in BDSM).

<u>Dominant</u>: the participant in charge of a kink interaction.

<u>D/s</u>: Domination and submission.

<u>Kink</u>: can mean an actual fetish, but can also refer to the broad panoply of BDSM and other "unusual" sexual activities.

<u>Safeword</u>: pre-arranged cue a participant can say to stop a BDSM activity that is too painful, too emotional, too much to handle.

<u>Scene</u>: a given session of BDSM activity.

<u>Submissive</u>: the participant who is not in charge during a kink interaction.

<u>Top</u>: the person on the giving end of an interaction (again, this is a down-and-dirty description; there's much more to this than topping, this is only a starting place).

<u>Vanilla</u>: sex that doesn't involve kink, fetishes, BDSM, etc.

Why kink?

First of all, why are you using kink or BDSM in the story? If you're just trying to hit an underserved market, but have no particular feel for kink yourself, that will probably come across in your writing and the BDSM elements will seem gratuitous. There's a slew of contemporary erotic romance novels right now that rely on fantasy-driven stereotypes about kink clubs and D/s, but completely ignore the dynamics of power exchange at the heart of that kind of relationship. Kink is not just a set of titillating activities, it's a mindset.

On the other hand, kink may well be a valuable component

in your book if you're hoping to highlight a complex relationship between your characters where power or deeply rooted emotional conflict are at issue. The BDSM can be a metaphor, helping to illustrate how a character feels constrained in his or her life, needs a push to reach a decision, needs or has lost control. The specific reason isn't as important as the fact that a reason must exist; *why kink* for these characters? Even if you start out just wanting to include it because you think it will sell, examine your book's themes and your character arcs, and see how the kink relates. Then expand on that relationship throughout the book. This will help you to develop your characters, the scenes will be richer and more emotionally resonant, and the story will benefit.

Try to avoid the cliché of characters being involved in BDSM because of childhood trauma or similar reasons. Of course some are involved in kink because of these things, and others are involved in kink despite these things, but on the whole it's a misconception that all people who enjoy BDSM do so because they are damaged or dysfunctional. Not every submissive has Daddy issues, not every Dominatrix is an abuse survivor...and very few Dominants are CEOs. Think outside the stereotypes, but remember the "reason" for your character's involvement in kink may just be that they like it. It feels good. It feels right. It's fun.

Look and Feel:

If you're determined to write kink into your sexy book, do it the right way. Do some research. If you haven't experienced an act you want to write about, you should at least be able to picture it in excruciating detail. You need to imagine how the parties feel before, during and after the activity—does this position put a lot of stress on particular joints, does this type of whip deliver "thud" or "sting", would the Dominant's arms get tired? Draw a sketch if that helps. Try it out in the privacy of your own home, if need be, using a pillow as a victim or testing out various positions for feasibility (if you have a partner who's willing to help you in these endeavors, all the better).

Find out what the real-life effects of a discipline session would be. Sometimes there's an assumption by the non-kinky that a sub is covered with bruises and other marks for days after each scene, and sometimes that's the case, but certainly not all the time or for every sub or Dom. You don't have to get close to damaging the skin to inflict a great deal of pain, and the human skin is tougher and more resilient than you might expect. Canes usually leave welts, as do single-tailed whips, but hand-spanking alone probably won't even leave visible signs by the next day (especially on an experienced sub) and even some floggers may not mark or bruise the skin in a lasting way. Paddles can leave stripes, reddened skin or bruises if used in certain ways, no lingering marks at all if used in others. On the other hand, biting and marking with the mouth (hickeys) usually does leave a bruise or other mark. Consider, too, whether your sub character bruises easily.

Is your Dominant in shape? Even so, a long session with a whip or flogger will tire out a shoulder, and spanking can sting the delivering hand nearly as much as the receiving bottom. Depending on the activity, your Dom may require a lot more athletic ability than your sub...but the sub is almost certainly more likely to need some flexibility. During and after the scene, who has muscle strain and where? Is it just annoying, or is it a pleasant reminder? Is it something the couple has to accommodate during the next scene?

Details like this really make the scene ring true for the reader. Setting details can do the same, which is why I highly encourage you to write BDSM that is *not* set in a kink club. BDSM isn't about clubs; it's about people, and more kink is practiced in the home than anywhere else. Does the heroine have ringbolts in her bed frame, suitable for attaching tethers? Does the husband's secret basement project turn out to be a spanking horse? What's in that demure heroine's bedside table drawer, and how does her girlfriend react when she finds out? Not only can these details be entertaining to write about, they can give you a lot of story fodder as you figure out how to introduce the kink realistically between your characters. The hero may have to do some groundwork if the heroine is to walk into his dungeon for the first time without freaking out.

In my book Tangled Truth, the hero is an expert at shibari (Japanese sensual rope bondage). By the time he reveals the binding points in *his* bed, however, he's already involved with the heroine and they've had vanilla sex once. The hero has her trust already by that time, and she's aware of his kinky proclivities for quite a while before he ties her up to have sex with her. Any earlier in the tale, and the trust element wouldn't have been established. In this story, by the way, the heroine is *refraining* from BDSM because of a bad early experience, and she wants to try again but is afraid. The ropes, for her, represent freedom—the freedom to express herself sexually by doing what feels good and right to her without shame.

Tangled Truth was fun for me to write, and easy in a way, because I have first-hand experience. This was critical, to me, for a story about rope bondage, because the feel of the rope is a key component of the attraction for the person being tied as well as the person doing the tying. However, anybody can go purchase some rope and do a bit of experimentation. Get a book about it (I highly recommend the Two Knotty Boys books), and look at the photos; what would the rope feel like, sliding *there* and pressing *there*? Put a rope there and find out, even if you can't do the whole complicated binding. Another thing to consider—how does the rope smell? Hemp in particular has a very distinctive smell (both the rope and the oils used to condition it), and that smell in itself can be arousing for a person who enjoys being tied. Conditioning occurs even when we don't mean for it to, and your character doesn't have to be aware of the conditioning for you to write about the effect; again, this sort of detail enriches the story and adds layers to your characterization and setting.

Just as important as the physical feel, however, is what the characters are thinking as they engage in kink. BDSM is not only about whips and chains (though they may excite you), or even about bondage and discipline. It's about the giving and taking of control. All the other stuff is just an external representation of that exchange. Characters may think about sex in ways that they wouldn't for vanilla sex, because of that symbolic aspect. It may mean a great deal more to them than simply expressing affection or doing something pleasurable.

There's a sort of trope in BDSM books—and in the kink community itself—that the submissive is the one with "all the control" because she/he can always safeword to stop the scene. While that may be true, it isn't necessarily foremost in a submissive's mind during a scene. A good Dominant can push a sub right up to that line, again and again, without going over it, but in general you're nowhere close to the safeword for most of any given scene. Veto power is not the same thing as control over the interaction, and most submissives wouldn't have it any other way because they don't want to be in control. They want the Dom to be in control; that's why they're subs. They don't want to safeword—although their reasons for that may vary wildly, and this can be another rich vein of internal conflict for the writer to mine.

Consider your sub's motivations, and do some research about that, too. What are the different "types" of subs? If the scene is very extreme, why does it still appeal to your sub? Does it still feel good enough to the sub to justify continuing on the basis of pleasure alone, and have you provided enough buildup for that to be a feasible motivation? Does the sub get off on pain, or on giving the Dom what he wants?

Is the sub in subspace, and do you know what that means? Another writer once asked me if it was a good idea to include subspace in a BDSM story written from the sub's point of view, but it was clear from her question that she didn't really know what subspace *was*. If you're a sub—or a runner who's experienced runner's high, which is a related phenomenon—then you may have firsthand experience of this. If you're not, you're going to have to do some research. Just know that subspace is not magic, it doesn't happen all the time or in every scene, and it doesn't happen at the beginning of an interaction. Again, it takes some groundwork from the Dom and sub alike, but you should see that as a source of material rather than a hindrance to your story. How does the Dom get the sub to that point?

An area I think bears more exploration in BDSM erotic romance is the mind of the Dominant. Too many times, a male Dom is cast as a CEO or billionaire entrepreneur, or a mysterious dark figure seen only in the kink club as "Master X". In real life, many Doms are guys who over think and overanalyze a lot—engineers and computer geeks (and most real-life female Dominants I know are often more interested in the psychology of the exchange than in wielding power as such; they're not women you would see in the grocery store and assume you're looking at a sexual Dominant). Male or female, the best Doms know—and use—the philosophy and physiology of BDSM to their advantage, much more than they rely on physical or monetary power. Your Dominant should be a thinking sort.

Your Dom should also have layers that the submissive doesn't necessarily see; the reader may like to know what's going on behind the Master's cool façade. The Dom in my book Roses and Chains is a newbie, and still has difficulty with self-control as well as knowing how to control his subs. His point of view includes a lot of self-talk as he figures out how to become the Master he wants to be, the Master he knows his subs need. He has doubts, he gets aroused at inconvenient times, he doesn't always know what he's "supposed" to do…but he knows the key is to pick a course of action and proceed as though he's confident, while still being flexible enough to change his plans to suit the situation if necessary. It's a delicate juggling act, and many readers have commented that they like reading his point of view and following his journey.

The Dom in Roses and Chains is hardly the typical romance-novel alpha male. He's an architect, a nerd, enjoys playing computer games, generally a nice guy and a good husband…and again, readers actively liked all that about him. An all-powerful arrogant CEO billionaire Dom can be great fun to read now and then, but don't think that's the only kind you can write. Try setting your BDSM in the real world, with real people.

Emotions and BDSM:

Another reason to place kink in the context of real-world interaction is the same reason I think many people in the real world enjoy BDSM in the first place: in addition to triggering more powerful physical releases, it may also trigger emotional releases that a kinkster doesn't experience with vanilla sex. Because of the nature of kink and its marginalization in our sexual culture, there is often a lot of emotion tied up in doing it at all, particularly at the beginning. Use that to your advantage as a writer. Is your character new to kink? Does he or she have long-suppressed urges about being bound or whipping somebody? Is there shame, fear, guilt? How does your top feel, and how does that differ from the bottom's perception going into the scene and coming out of it? Perhaps the characters are simply excited about the whole thing.

During the scene, characters who are used to vanilla sex may be surprised to find themselves having strong emotional reactions as the tension and arousal rises. Pain and endorphin release can cause the mind to play tricks, but can also cause us to lower our own internal defenses against things that are troubling us; consider the possibility that the kink is in some way providing catharsis for your character. Then consider how that catharsis affects the Dom. A new Dom might be anxious to find his sub suddenly in tears; an experienced Dom, on the other hand, won't be surprised by that type of reaction and might even have reassurance for the sub (yes, a Dom can be reassuring and even gentle to a sub during a scene, it all depends on the characters).

What is going through your characters' minds after the scene? Another research topic should be "aftercare", and you should consider the possibility that your Dom may need some aftercare as well as your sub. Even a sub who wants to feel degraded and humiliated during a scene will want to be reassured afterward, usually; and even a Dom who maintains an icy cruelty for the scene's sake probably wants to know after that scene that the sub doesn't think he's an asshole.

This is another way in which real life BDSM so often differs from erotic romance novels, because the novels often skimp on aftercare. The roles in aftercare can differ so sharply from the stereotypical Dom and sub categories that it's sometimes difficult to make those scenes believable for your characters. Again, though, it's a potential source for material to make your characters deeper and more interesting. You should also take advantage of the chance to give your readers some aftercare, by helping them see how the characters debrief after the scene, so they can transition back into the non-sexual parts of the story line more easily.

That brings me to another factor in using BDSM in erotic romance novels. Just as in any book, the sex shouldn't stop the story line or the character arc. If anything, the sex is when a lot of the character development should take place. In particular it's when the relationship development takes place, and the sex becomes a metaphor for the way the characters interact with each other outside the bedroom. The characters are the most like themselves in those moments, and the heat of the moment takes the blinders off them, allowing insights that have been evading them. If it's done right, the sex doesn't seem gratuitous. Kink can make that dichotomy between everyday thinking and flashes of emotional insight even more extreme, but the kinky sex should still serve the story and not the other way around.

Final Thoughts:

Strange though it may be to hear this from somebody who writes kinky erotic romance, my advice is to think of yourself as writing a story first, a romance second, an erotic romance third, and a kinky book only fourth (if at all). Even if your stated goal is to write a BDSM erotic romance, you must have a story and, unless you're writing erotica, that story must satisfy the conventions of romance novels. Sex may figure prominently in your novel, but if it's to be BDSM-oriented sex you need to justify that. It needs to make sense and even serve a purpose in your story. Otherwise, the reader may be titillated but she won't be engaged.

The danger is that BDSM can get complicated, and statistically speaking any given erotic romance writer probably hasn't done all the acts she's writing about. And some percentage of readers will be able to tell, because they *have* done that act. Those readers probably won't be back if the scenes don't ring true to them. *So do your research.* Work the kink into the storyline as an integral component, not a sexy decoration. Remember that kinky people are still *real* people, and their bodies and minds have the same limitations anybody else has. Your character may get a cramp from that tricky suspension bondage…but that's okay, it will make the scene more real and it will make your book better. Maybe your Dom has doubts; seeing how he overcomes those will make him or her more interesting to the reader.

Actions don't make the kinkster; thoughts do. You can have a vanilla sex scene with spanking, set in a dungeon festooned with whips and chains, and you can have a kinky sex scene in a tastefully decorated suburban bedroom with no props at all and only missionary-style sex. It all depends on what the characters are thinking and feeling, which is why a writer must do the research into these hidden aspects of kink if the scenes are to read true. The payoff is a deep, complex relationship between characters whose layers will fascinate your readers and keep them coming back for more.

Delphine Dryden wants you to stay in touch!
Website (writing): DelphineDryden.com
Website (editing): TheEditorHat.com
Twitter: Twitter.com/deldryden
Tumblr: deldryden.tumblr.com
Facebook: facebook.com/DelphineDryden
Goodreads: goodreads.com/delphinedryden
Email: author@delphinedryden.com

12
BIOLOGY: THE GOOD, THE BAD, & THE SEX SCENE
BY JEAN JOHNSON

About Jean Johnson:

Jean is a national & *New York Times* bestselling author of erotica, romance, & science fiction. She's been published with Berkley, Ace, Flying Pen Press, translated and internationally published with Blanvalet & Penhaligon (RandomHouse.de), and published online with CrossedGenres.com.

Reviewers have said "Jean Johnson's writing is fabulously fresh, thoroughly romantic, and wildly entertaining. Terrific—fast, sexy, charming, and utterly engaging. I loved it!"—*New York Times* bestselling author Jayne Ann Krentz, and "A must read for those who enjoy fantasy and romance...Jean Johnson can't write them fast enough for me!"—*The Best Reviews*

Jean Johnson can read most text upside-down, mirror-reversed, & even upside-down-reversed, though that last one takes her a little while. Her penmanship, however, has puzzled even professional pharmacists for many years—yay for typing!

Biology:
The Good, The Bad, & the Sex Scene
by Jean Johnson

Greetings, students!

I am your course instructor, Jean Johnson, and I've been writing erotic and romantic literature for many years now, including award-winning fanfics, erotica at Literotica, and fantasy romance novels through Berkley Sensations. Welcome to my writing class on Biology: The Good, The Bad, & The Sex Scene.

…Settle down, please; I know this is a very popular topic for obvious reasons, but we have a lot to get through, today. Please try not to giggle too much, because you will want to take notes and will thus want to listen carefully—and as a lot of you sneak in here even though you aren't on the official course roster, I'll just skip taking roll call and move right into the topic for today's class.

This is a writing course which aims to prevent you from making unfortunate mistakes in your fiction when writing out a sex scene, and which will hopefully teach you how to write better ones, once you are armed with some pertinent facts. The reason why it falls under the Biology heading is because most everything I am going to teach you today is related directly to the biology of the typical, average human being. Or two beings, rather, since I'll be discussing both male and female physiology.

Why We Write About Sex

First of all, most of us like sex…please, students, hold the giggling to a minimum? We're all adults, here. What I'm trying to say is, most of us have tried it and most of us have found at least some level of enjoyment for it above a mere tolerance level. Of course, an unfortunate number of us have found ourselves composing grocery lists or whatever at certain points during lovemaking, but part of that simply stems from either ourselves or our partners not really knowing how to stimulate our bodies enough to make our brains shut up, hang on, and enjoy the ride.

A quick reminder, students, before we delve into the topic of arousal itself: The single most potent sexual organ in the human body is the brain. Stimulate the brain as well as the body, and I guarantee that you will rock that person's world far more than if you just stimulated the exact body parts. Literature is one of the best ways to stimulate the brain, particularly for females, which is why romance books are so popular.

Once we discover the pleasure inherent in our bodies, sexual thoughts and feelings do tend to intrigue us; the pursuit of pleasure is akin to the pursuit of happiness. We also know from experience that sharing pleasure increases pleasure for both partners. Unfortunately, we aren't always in a position where we have a loving partner on hand for, well, some loving. So when people want to experience those physical and emotional rushes associated with lovemaking, we turn to various types of entertainment media.

Writing erotic prose is one of the best ways to give others the chance to have that shared-pleasure experience. It is different from porn in that there is usually some sort of plot, engaging the reader's interest above and beyond copulation; it involves the reader's emotions more than straightforward porn—erotic romance involves even more of the emotional side of things, pleasing the reader's brain as well as their body.

Of course, videos are pretty blatant about what they are, but if you tried to watch one on your mobile device while riding the bus, you could get into trouble. Erotic writing, however, is both portable and discreet. It permits you to attain a state of excitement without being blatant, and it stimulates your single most important sexual organ, your mind.

Arousal
The first thing you need to understand is that there is a

huge difference between the genders when it comes to physical arousal…and I'm not just talking erections, here. If you want to be 100% accurate, females can and do get erections just the same as males. It is only that their equipment, the clitoris, nipples, even the swelling of breast and vulva tissues, are far less blatantly visible than a man's penis becoming erect.

We can write passages such as, *She didn't expect her skin to shiver from the feel of his hand on her forearm; her knee, maybe, since her legs had always been a bit sensitive, but no, he was arousing her with the simplest touch of palm on skin. When he slid that hand to her elbow, lightly guiding her into the restaurant, she felt her nipples tighten beneath her dress, aching with the need to be suckled by that perpetually half-amused mouth of his.* But in order to pull it off believably, we need to do what Mark Twain told a young Jack London at the start of his writing career: "Write what you know."

If you want to write believable, enthralling erotica, it really helps to know what you're talking about. With that in mind, I want to talk about arousal itself.

Arousal, the state of physical and psychological excitation in which the body and the mind prepare themselves for copulation and pleasure-seeking, shares a very odd yet very understandable connection to our fight-or-flight instincts. Whether it's sex or combat, it all comes down to the fact that we are biological beings with a gene-deep imperative to procreate and survive.

However, whichever committees designed human beings did not consult each other on these methods when it comes to the differences in arousal between the genders. Most specifically, I mean the timing of the adrenaline-arousal spikes.

Everyone knows that males are more likely to get aroused quickly, and that females take longer to get there. This is because arousal follows pretty much the same curve as the adrenaline spike we get when we face a potential fight.

If you'll look at the main screen behind me, you'll see a series of examples I've written to illustrate how these things work in storytelling. First up, the adrenaline version:

***

Greg knew they were going to hit him. He had come here to Tony's Body Shop to apologize for not having the money to pay off his "special loan" and he knew Big Mike and Half-Pipe Pete were going to hit him as soon as he finished explaining things to their boss, Tony. He also knew he wasn't going to go down without a fight. As the words tumbled out of his mouth faster and faster, as he explained about his grandmother's heart surgery and her insurance company's refusal to pay the bills, his whole frame tensed, ready to kick or block or duck. It all depended on whether or not he could evoke some shred of human compassion in the tiny dot that passed for the crime lord's heart, but he wasn't going to hold his breath.

***

And now the arousal story:

***

When did Gloria develop such a magnificent ass? Greg didn't know, but he hoped she spent several more minutes digging around in the cupboards under the counter of the office breakroom. For a moment he wondered what he'd ever seen in apple-round breasts, when here were a pair of perfectly presented cantaloupes jiggling and straining against the fabric. For a moment, he could see it in his mind, stripped bare and lightly blushed with a hint of a spank or two…the ultimate office fantasy, since Gloria was his temporary boss on this assignment, and wasn't bashful about ordering *him* around.

***

Writing about arousal creates tension in a scene, just as writing about adrenaline does. However, males and females go about it in two separate ways, and it's based in our biology.

Male Arousal

For men, imagine a graph of their arousal. The curve on the graph rises sharply over about a minute and a half, peaks, and then tapers off over a period of about ten minutes. This is the same spike as fight-or-flight adrenaline rush males get when they meet the intruder at the front door, and either scare him off—and calm down again quickly—or fight fast and hard to keep him out. He'll shoot a gun once, maybe twice if he missed.

As you can see, men are quick to arouse, and quick to cool down. A man can back down from a fight anywhere up to within a few seconds of the peak. Backing down from sexual arousal is a little more difficult simply because all that rushing blood is being pumped into one constricted region, and once the various hormones are released, they don't vanish instantaneously upon command...but again, not impossible.

...Sorry, guys, but I'm here to tell the ladies that you men will not "die" when suffering from blue-balls. Unless you're suffering from priapism, which is a prolonged and painful penile erection lasting more than a few hours—you've all heard the erectile pill disclaimers regarding the four hour timeframe, right? If you do suffer from that, go see a doctor immediately, as it can be medically dangerous. But I digress. "Blue balls" isn't an actual fatal disease, so please stop trying to convince your partners it is...and stop trying to write it into your stories as such.

If nothing else, we writers can always have our extremely aroused male protagonists excuse himself to go to the bathroom for a few minutes, where he can take care of the problem in private. Additionally, after the first climax, a man's adrenal/arousal response system slows down, so "taking the edge off" a man is a perfectly normal method of helping make sure his pleasure is attended to so he can have a clear head for focusing on his lady's own delights.

Writing a scenario like this makes it easier to help build some of that important sexual tension. For example:

***

That down-the-blouse peak at Gloria's perfect breasts, with her nipples straining against the sheer pink fabric of her bra, had him blushing and muttering a hasty excuse about eating too much chili last night. Shutting the bathroom door, Greg barely remembered to lock it with a fumble of his left hand. The right one was already cupping his groin, as if in futile effort to confine the pleasure throbbing through his flesh. Unable to think of anything else, he quickly unfastened his slacks and gripped his shaft, stroking in time to his racing heartbeat.

All he could think about was marching back out there and seeing if it really was possible to pop buttons off a blouse with just one's teeth. It would be employment suicide if they were caught, but oh, so sweet. And if he had the chance to actually taste her breasts—if they tasted anything like the vanilla perfume she wore...well, warm, sweet vanilla would instantly supplant chocolate chip mint on his list of favorite treats. Head braced against the door panel, body straining into the fast pumping of his hand, Greg strangled his usual long groan down into a brief, low grunt as he came.

***

As you can see, men can be aroused quickly. But because they can also back off easily, sometimes the system gets shut down prematurely or mucked up somewhere along the signaling pathways, and they suffer from erectile dysfunction. Now in the earlier years of an adult male's life, visual stimulation is often enough, but in his later years, a man sometimes needs a literal helping hand to stimulate the nerves directly and get the blood flowing for an erection—the other drawback to aging is that after his physical peak, a man often cannot achieve more than one erection and ejaculation in a night.

This is nothing to be ashamed of, gentlemen. The effects of aging and erectile dysfunction happen to nearly every man at some point in his life. Stress can trigger it, physical ailments can be a part of it, exhaustion or an ongoing argument or a million other things can make it happen. There are ways to work through the situation...and there are ways to stimulate and pleasure a man without involving just the penis. But that's a subject for later. For now, go see your doctors, keep yourselves healthy, exercise—this goes for women, too. The healthier and happier you are, the better your sex lives will be.

Remember also that whatever applies to *you* also applies to your characters. The above scene in the bathroom could be turned around so that our protagonist, Greg, suffers from erectile dysfunction. The reasons why could be many. Perhaps Greg is still stressed over medical bills, and is just too tense to achieve release, leaving him with a hard-on which diminishes from frustration. Maybe his cell phone goes off and it's a call from Tony the crime boss wanting to discuss alternate payment plans, causing an instant, worry-based deflation. Or maybe he simply has a fetish and needs to picture Gloria in bondage gear before he can get his rocks off.

This is where putting plot into your stories elevates your descriptions from pornography to erotic prose.

Female Arousal

As for females and the adrenaline/arousal curve, this is where I wish the biological design teams working on the two genders had communicated with each other a bit more clearly. Why, you may ask? Because while a man can get aroused, peak, and calm down in an average of ten minutes…it takes an average of ten minutes just for a woman to reach her peak, followed by another fifty minutes of plateauing and gradual tapering off before she finally calms down.

Women spike their adrenaline about ten minutes or so because in the above example with the intruder, they're waiting back in the kitchen or the bedroom, having listened to their mate trying to fight off that intruder for the last several minutes. By the time that idiotic intruder finally makes it to them, the female is now most likely the last line of defense between her attacker and her children. She will not only fire the gun, she'll empty the entire clip of bullets into her intruder because she's literally so worked up, she can't calm down or back down from that survival instinct adrenaline spike as fast as a man can.

Again, we'll use two examples of adrenaline and arousal writing. This time, the writing is from the female perspective. First, the adrenaline rush:

***

Gloria couldn't believe Greg had dragged her into this mess. First the sob story about his grandmother's heart condition—however true—and now this bastard Tony and his two goons were trying to duke it out with Greg. Watching Greg defending himself with a duck and a block and a couple of wild swings of his own, she flinched back into the corner of the room, next to the coat stand and the umbrella holder. Her thigh bumped the curved handle of an old-fashioned umbrella in the holder, still damp from the morning rain. Snatching it out of the bin, she clutched it in front of her, psyching herself up to defend herself if this crime boss decided he wanted to use her as bystander leverage against her friend. If he did try, he and his goons would have to do it with an umbrella jabbed through an eye, or maybe their throats, or...or...

***

And now the arousal scene:

***

Smirking, Gloria pretended to rummage through the storage cupboards a bit more, though she had already found the paperwork forms he needed to start filling out. She knew he was checking out her butt; she'd seen the focus of his gaze through the curtain of her hair. Being placed in a position of authority over him, however temporary, was a heady thing. Greg was the office hottie; rumor had it he kick-boxed to keep in shape, and the way his shirts clung to his frame had hinted at gorgeous muscles. If he wanted to stare at her ass, she'd let him; it was only fair. She'd been discreetly ogling his for the last six weeks.

***

As you can see, Greg is thinking about the actual moment, whether it's adrenaline or arousal. He wants to act now. Gloria has been building up to her emotional/hormonal rush, taking more time, though with no less intensity in the end.

An example of our heroine growing aroused over time could be played out over several paragraphs, several pages, or several hours or days of in-story time as the sexual tension between the two ratchets up. She could even wake up in the morning in the story, anticipating her hot date with the hero later that night. When writing from your heroine's POV (point of view), you can show exactly how she feels her body getting turned on. The way her bra feels tight—in other words, her breasts and nipples are swelling—or maybe by the way she has to cross her legs and cannot sit still—her clitoris, vulva and labia are becoming engorged and sensitive—or she can fantasize about what it'll be like when she finally does get him into bed or wherever. Perhaps even the office supply closet, who knows? This is also a good time to take a look at the protagonists' surroundings and figure out which locations could be used for a tryst. Let your—and your character's—imagination run wild.

Women, too, can suffer from the equivalent of erectile dysfunction. Since it does take several minutes more for women to become fully aroused, this process can be interrupted at any point along the way by anything. An actual interruption, "Oh my god, my mother's calling!" or a sudden reversal of fortune, "Ewww, his breath stinks of liver and onions! I can't kiss him when it smells like that!" or it could have a biological basis. It's the wrong time of month, or she has a cold, her health isn't good, she has the clichéd headache, whatever. These, too, can be written into a scene.

The Timing and Value of Written Arousal

Now, let me repeat this information, because it's very important when it comes to writing sex scenes: Adrenaline and arousal follow the same curves, per gender. Men get aroused, peak, plateau, and calm down over a period of about ten minutes, unless they train their bodies to respond differently. Women take a full ten minutes just to get to their peak, and then spend the rest of an hour enjoying themselves before finally calming down.

This biological disparity, if you'll pardon my vulgarity, is utterly fucked up. Laugh all you like, students; it's still a fact. If we *write* sex strictly by the timing of these arousal spikes, then by the time a woman is finally ready to enjoy herself, her man has already done the deed and is snuggling into the bedding for a nap, or craving a beer, whatever.

This is also one of the biggest reasons why in the real world, so many women have reported difficulty in achieving orgasm…yet that same woman can spend half an hour reading a romance novel, and find herself very much "in the mood."

However, do not think this fault is laid solely at the feet of our partners. Some of it does lie in whether or not a male cares enough to be patient in helping to arouse the female, but that's not everything. It also depends on whether or not the female has enough foresight to start preparing herself mentally and physically to be aroused and ready for her male. This is therefore far more the flaw of timing than one of his-or-her responsibility.

Most of us are now programmed via our fast-paced, fast-changing world to expect near-instant results. Immediate gratification. I can cook a microwave dinner faster than the amount of time it takes my female biology to reach the peak of readiness for sexual gratification. Like I said, the design specs are fucked up. If a woman wants to be aroused, she has to spend several minutes turning her thoughts towards the pleasures of sex, even if she's simply intending a solo session. She has to concentrate on it…and as we all know, it's far too easy to break our concentration in today's world of distractions. Men can be aroused more quickly than that, but a minute and a half is only the average, and like women, anything can interrupt the process of arousal

Still, it can be done, and it's usually worthwhile. Recently, I read an interesting scientific study speculating on one of the reasons why humans may have evolved into such socially sentient beings. The researchers suggested the screwed-up timing difference could have actually arisen from the male's need to slow down and take the time to arouse the female more fully, giving the couple more time to form a caring partner-bond. In other words, the more time a man takes to arouse and ensure the enjoyment of his lover, the more likely she'll want to continue to have sex with him again, so on and so forth, until the pair have bonded together in preference for mates.

Now, what has all of this to do with writing believable sex scenes? Writing good sex isn't just about getting our rocks off. That's very much a part of it—but writing good sex scenes is also about instructing our readers. Indeed, many of us first learned about sex through romance books…mainly because our parents were more careful about monitoring all other forms of information streams reaching our tender little eyes and ears.

Yes, yes, I see several hands raised, and I can guess what most of you are about to point out: Aren't sex videos a valid form of instruction? Yes, and no. Yes, because you can see how the bodies fit together—and the discussion on Why That Particular Position Won't Work During Sex is another class topic in and of itself. The "no" part comes into play because the thing you have to remember about sex videos is that the vast majority are marketed toward men. Remember men, who peak in about a minute and a half? Yeah. They're marketed at men, which means plotted for men, and that means in most videos, the sexual action will start happening within the first few minutes for many of them. Many, but not all.

This disparity can be seen most clearly within two types of videos. If you watch sex videos featuring two groups of homosexual couples—real couple videos, not just professional industry actors—the sex between the male pair will be quicker, the peaks will build faster. Everything seems more intense. Between the two females, it will build slower, be more sensual, but it will also be intense by the time they reach the end. If you examine some of the rare sex videos marketed for women, you'll see that the sexual tension is scripted out so that it takes place over a longer time, to better match a woman's biological arousal timetable.

…No, students, I'm not going to recommend specific videos to any of you, and no, I'm not going to hand out extra credit points if you go forth and research those things. You can do that on your own time. This class is about writing great sex, not filming great sex. I merely use the videos as an example to help clarify matters further.

The main difference between the two formats is that while videos are targeted for a primarily male purchasing and viewing audience, books are more likely to be bought and read by women. Indeed, the vast majority of romance novels are written by women for women, and a clear majority of erotica novels are read by women, particularly those in the sub-category referred to by the erotic romance powerhouse Ellora's Cave as "Romantica".

Yes, you there in the middle, toward the left? What's the difference between romance and erotica? Well, I'm glad you asked that, because that is a very good question.

Romance Versus Erotica

Romance focuses primarily on building a relationship between two people. The amount of sex can vary, anywhere from a chaste kiss or hug all the way through to bondage and domination if that's the story's kink. But the primary focus, the primary plot driving the story, is the mental and emotional relationship. Erotica focuses primarily on the sexual relationship. There may be a fairly decent love story building throughout a particular erotic tale, but not always.

So! Now that we know there are arousal timing differences between the two genders, and that the time a gentleman takes to warm up his lady partner to the idea of great sex is very much a biological necessity, let us open our textbooks to review specific instances of male and female arousal as written into a particular sex scene in published works. Our little impromptu paragraphs about Greg and Gloria are okay as far as short little vignettes go, but writing erotica is about putting together a whole story, not just snippets and passages taken mostly out of context.

Remember, the more you can weave erotic writing into a whole story, the more your readers are going to enjoy it on many levels, since the brain is our biggest, most important erogenous zone. It's like the difference between straightforward intercourse, and taking the time to arouse your partner properly: the short version might get the job done, but you'll have a much more enjoyable time if you take the time and make the effort to arouse everything that you can.

Erotica in Novels

Writing an erotic novel is different than writing snippets of erotica. This is because if your happy couple are in the middle of a big fight scene with Tony and his goons Big Mike and Half-Pipe Pete...they're not going to suddenly stop fighting the goons and start making out on the spot. It just makes no sense. That sort of thing might get published as a poorly written porn story mailed in to some sleazy "letters" magazine, but this is erotica, a much more coherent level of writing. To that end, we will study how you can successfully put erotica into an actual story.

The first book we'll reference is my novel *The Sword*, originally released by Berkley Sensations in 2007. We start with the first scene of Chapter 6. ...Ready? Good.

Here, we have a scene where our hero Saber is contemplating a brief but salacious glimpse at the nether-parts of our heroine Kelly. He contemplates her visual charms, remembering the feel of her body, and in general mentally stimulates—even torments—himself with thoughts of her and the possibility of sleeping with her. She's not even in the same room, and he knows at this point in the story it's just too dangerous to risk the prophesied disaster that would occur if he claimed her...but he still takes himself in hand and masturbates. This is a very male train of thought, and a very male pattern of stimulation, direct and to the point. He may stretch it out, but he's not likely to spend a full hour in this activity.

When Kelly takes a few moments in turn to contemplate Saber's physical appeal, she briefly caresses herself as she does so. She does not, however, work herself up to a state of completion. Even though Saber has been sent on the task of finding suitable paraphernalia for her to have a nice bath— fetching towels, soaps, and so forth—and is presumed to be gone for at least ten minutes since they're staying in a large, half-abandoned palace, she knows she doesn't have enough time to stimulate herself to a climax.

She does, however, bank those feelings like banking the embers in a fire. Implicitly, the heroine intends to keep them still burning and thus ready to be fanned up into flames later on when she does have the time to take care of her own sexual needs. It isn't openly written in the narrative that she does masturbate to thoughts of him, but it is implied directly by her own words, which we can see at the end of Chapter Eleven. There are, of course, other notable sex scenes in this novel, but we'll turn instead to your second course book, *The Cat*, released by Berkley Sensations 2008 in the trade paperback edition, and 2009 in the mass market.

Here Trevan and Amara are once again flirting with each other, this time in his workroom. He is trying to be respectful of her culture's "not before marriage" attitude toward sex, whereas she is attempting to adapt to his own local culture's more causal "anything goes between adults, so long as you have a contraceptive amulet" approach.

Trevan is portrayed as a sexually experienced gentleman, having enjoyed many partners in his past. With his years of experimentation and practice, he understands the value of staving off a quick climax in favor of a slower build and a stronger pleasure payoff for both partners. Still, as the sexual tension in the room rises, we see in just a few short pages that her efforts to examine and arouse him have a strong effect, and he climaxes. It happens a bit precipitously when compared to his experience and self-control, but mostly because the sexual tension between the two protagonists is written so strongly.

Trevan then devotes a lot of time and effort to preparing Amara for pleasure. She is already aroused by this point, having enjoyed her experimentations on him in the preceding pages, but he takes his time to caress and stimulate various parts of her body anyway, until she finally climaxes. As does he, a few moments later.

By the way, it is not necessary for your characters to constantly have mutual simultaneous climaxes. This is actually a rare occurrence in real life. It can happen, particularly when the female is still on her post-peak plateau arousal high, making her capable of more orgasms when properly stimulated, but feel free to stagger the pleasure in your partners. This injects a note of realism which your readers will appreciate.

Remember, students, we have a responsibility as writers to instruct our readers as much as we mentally stimulate. Unrealistic expectations gleaned from escapism literature may lead to real-life disappointments when too many unfavorable or unattainable comparisons are being made. Put some realism back into your stories—yes, people do have to stop and use the bathroom once in a while, mid-sex—and people will be relieved to know it is possible to attain such pleasures in their own love-lives.

Now, backing up a little bit, let's look at a scene earlier in *The Cat* that shows Trevan successfully seducing Amara by the strict courting customs of her own cultural background. I draw your attention to it, students, because of the fact that variety is not only the spice of life, it can often become a necessity, particularly in something as frequently occurring as sex, when one is in a healthy adult relationship.

What do I mean by that? Well, picture if you will a cat. Yes, yes, feel free to laugh, given the title of the course book we're currently examining. But bear with me, and picture a common, ordinary housecat.

If you pet the cat in a proper, gentle fashion, the cat will enjoy it and purr. You can pet the cat for quite a while this way, using the same strokes of your hand over and over. However, there will come a point in time where either the cat will grow bored of the same old thing over and over, or even grow irritated by the constant, unvaried stimulation. It is therefore best to vary up your strokes, maybe petting a flank as well as the spine, scratching behind the ears or under the chin, rubbing the base of the tail, so on and so forth.

The same can be said for sex. Vary your sexual activities, and you will avoid both boredom and the potential for irritation. Caress each other in different areas, pursue different levels of stimulation, experiment with different positions, and don't be afraid to try new things. You can go back to the favorites, but do change it up. If your readers can predict what sexual moves will happen when in your next novel, based on the last four or five you've written being all the same, then it's definitely time to throw them a curveball in the very next scene.

So in this earlier scene, we see Trevan surmounting the challenge of Amara's culture. He very carefully does not touch her breasts or her groin directly. He does not even kiss her. But by using his breath, her own body positions, and his words and self-confidence as his tools, he manages to stimulate her to a minor climax. Mostly by seducing her brain as well as her body, and he does it while both of them are fully clothed.

Let me tell you, having had this done to me by a very confident man was just as stimulating, personally. It also opened my eyes up to all the various possibilities of sexual encounters that exist out there, redefining my senses of sexuality and sensuality, both as a woman and as a writer—and I say both because it is a truism that we should try to write what we ourselves know. That means you may want to try different things first-hand to see what does or does not work.

…Okay, students, put your hands down. I am not going to assign "find a sexual partner and experiment with them" as part of your course curriculum or homework. That is something you can do on your own time for your own reasons.

I'm here to teach the lot of you how to write out a good, erotically charged sex scene, not how to live out one.

Stimulation

Speaking of which, each human being, male and female, is different when it comes to stimulating arousal. You've all heard the phrases, "I'm a tits man," or, "I'm an ass man," when it comes to men. Some like the visual stimulation, others prefer tactile. Some prefer certain smells and tastes. Women aren't much different when it comes to the mental side of arousal. Different things will set them off, depending upon the individual, so please take in all of this with the understanding that there will always be exceptions to the rule.

On the other hand, men and women differ physically in their erogenous hot-spots, mainly because men have one obvious one, being the penis, and women have two less obvious ones, being the external clitoris and the internal Gräfenberg spot (aka the G-spot). Stroke the shaft of a man's penis and he will usually get excited. This stroking is a physiological response to stimulation which simulates the thrusting of the penis into the vagina; it's literally telling the body, "Heyyy, I'm copulating, isn't that grand?"

For women…again, the design specs are a bit messed up. The greatest sexual stimulation organ we females have is the clitoris, which only rarely comes into contact with the male body during standard intercourse, unless you vary the positions just so, or you resort to additional stimulation on top of actual intercourse—good sex is always about more than just intercourse.

There is nothing wrong with having to do this manually; again, it comes down to the idea that if your partner takes the time to stimulate you during sex, you'll be so happy with him that, next chance you get, you'll be more likely to pick the partner who did physically please you. This helps to build intimacy in relationships, whether real or fictional. The clitoris has the single greatest concentration of nerve-endings in the entire female body—more even than the male, inch for inch—

so stimulating this spot is your best bet to please a lady.

The other common climactic spot is the Gräfenberg spot, or G-spot. It does exist in women, and is analogous to the prostate gland in men. However, it is much more difficult to find, more difficult to stimulate, and isn't nearly as sensitive regarding pleasure in most women as the clitoris itself. If you are one of the lucky women, forty percent or less, who enjoy such stimulation, do feel free to enjoy it. If you're one of the smaller percentage who enjoy both, or at least whose partners have managed to find both and can stimulate them properly, congratulations!

On an amusing side-note, the two most popular methods of stimulating the clitoris and the G-spot are known in certain circles as the "Hello" and "Come Here" methods. "Hello" is often depicted as fingers toward your partner, hand moving in a circular wave motion, literally rubbing the clit, whereas "Come Here" is depicted as holding your palm toward yourself, your first one or two fingers stroking towards yourself in a beckoning motion. If your lady-partner is lying on her back, the application of these two methods is very self-evident, particularly since that'll ensure your fingers are at least rubbing on the correct wall of her vagina, and might have a chance at finding the right spot.

For most gentlemen, the most stimulating part of the shaft is the spot known as the frenulum. If you look at the head of the penis, you will see a ridge circling most of the head. Where it sweeps upward to a point on the underside, that point-area is commonly called the frenulum—or *frenulum preputti penis* in Latin—and contains the most number of sexual nerve endings for men. Other areas may be exciting, and of course a gentleman's prostate can be gently massaged if he'll let you stick a finger or two in his "backdoor" for an often fantastic effect…but like most women and the clitoris, it's the frenulum that makes most guys' legs turn to goo.

Copulation Caveats
Do not, however, go straight for these final erogenous

spots, whether in real life or in your writing. Explore in different directions. Write more than just tits-and-ass scenes. For example, having someone lick your inner elbow or wrist can be quite arousing—this is not something your reader will be expecting, but they will find it stimulating. A lot of women also get turned on by a good foot or back rub. And most men find having their earlobe suckled to be overwhelmingly intense, so it's not just about penises and clitorises. We have the whole body to play with, as consensual adults.

As in real life, so in writing, whether you're writing about Greg and Gloria who live and work in Atlanta, or Zibnor and Tikla, furry felinoid creatures who live and make love on the planet Rabulaxx. Oh, and if you're going to write about erotica in non-human biologies, be consistent in your descriptions of how arousal works, and try not to be so outlandish that your readers have no clue what's going on, if you want your story to have actual erotic elements. What we understand, we can empathize with, so make sure your readers can understand what's happening.

Start with the little things and work your way up: spotting a nice ass, a sexy-confident smile, the smell of a leather jacket; a touch of the hand, a kiss, nibbling on necklines and fingertips; tracing patterns on exposed bits of skin, rubbing sore feet, exploring the borderline between stocking tops and bare skin; the first glimpse of naked flesh, cupping breasts and buttocks, maybe a scene where they're bathing together…

As you can see, each phase of eroticism in the above list builds up to the next level. Use this technique in your writing, whether it takes you five sentences, five paragraphs, or five pages to get to the "good stuff."

In fact, I'll tell you the single most important fact of biology: Men *can* slow down and take their time getting aroused, just like women. They don't have to be over and done with after just a minute and a half. When they do take their time, the experience is still just as intense for them, if not more so. After all, the object of erotica isn't to rush to the finish line as fast as you can. That's pornography. Erotica is all about enjoying the ride for however long you can make it last.

Whatever we can do within the framework of our biologies in real life, we can put that into our stories, making them feel more real. If we engage our readers' senses through descriptions involving sight, sound, smell, touch, and taste, we can engage their own arousal mechanisms, giving them a good time through our prose. And remember, stimulating the brain as well as the body will make that good time into a great time, and bring your readers back for more, more, more.

Now, students, armed with these facts of biology at your fingertips, you should be ready to write realistic sex scenes in your own manuscripts. For further reading, I recommend the entire Sons of Destiny series if you like long stories that focus on the plot as well as the smut, and not just *The Sword* and *The Cat*, books 1 and 5 respectively in that series.

I also recommend *Bedtime Stories* for excellent examples of short-length erotica, along with *Finding Destiny* and *The Shifting Plains*. I do not, however, recommend reading *A Soldier's Duty* in your search for further literary lessons on well-written erotica, as the only thing hardcore about that particular book series is that it's hardcore military science fiction. Information on where to find these books can be found at www.JeanJohnson.net. If you have any questions, I can be reached via my website, and at JeanJAuthor on Twitter, or through Fans of Author Jean Johnson on Facebook.

...With all that said, I see that our time is now up. Please remember to return any borrowed books to the library, don't forget to check your auditorium seats to make sure you have all your belongings, and as always, try to practice safe, mutually consensual sex with an equally of-age partner whenever you may chose to do so. Oh, and if you want to play with the scenarios suggested in the Greg and Gloria storyline, feel free to do so; these examples were merely snippets. The whole of their story can be imagined by each one of you, if you choose.

Stay safe, and have fun writing about all that hot sex.

Jean Johnson wants you to stay in touch!
Website: JeanJohnson.net
Blog: JeanJauthor.tumblr.com
Twitter: twitter.com/JeanJAuthor
Facebook: http://tinyurl.com/3pvqk9y
Goodreads: http://bit.ly/phBv8A
Email: JeanJohnson.author@yahoo.com

13
RX FOR A SAGGY LOVE SCENE
BY CARI QUINN

About Cari Quinn

Cari Quinn is a *USA Today*, Amazon, and Barnes and Noble bestselling erotic romance author. She's published with Entangled Publishing, Samhain, Ellora's Cave, Loose Id, The Wild Rose Press, and her own co-owned self-publishing imprint, Rainbow Rage Publishing.

Reviewers have said Cari Quinn "…certainly made it to my auto-buy list because her books are seriously way over the hot, hot zone packaged with a ton of emotion that I as a romance reader absolutely revel in." – Maldivian Book Reviewer

Though Cari loves fall, it's not because it's football season (she much prefers basketball!) She also loves Starbucks' Pumpkin Spice Lattes, Halloween, and curling up to write and read sexy tales on a chilly autumn night.

Rx for a Sagging Sex Scene
by Cari Quinn

As anyone who writes sex knows, it can be a challenge to keep the tension high and the action steamy while also advancing the story. Not to mention occasionally needing new nuts to spice up the same old coffeecake, if you catch my drift.

I've got some tips I think will help make your romance writing the best it can be. So what makes me an expert? (Or sexpert, if the title fits?) So far I've been published with three erotic ebook publishers: The Wild Rose Press, Loose Id and Ellora's Cave. I've also been part of a self-published erotic romance anthology with three other multi-published authors. Later this year, The Wild Rose Press will be publishing my eighth erotic romance. All of my books published thus far have been erotic contemporaries, all m/f, though my latest Ellora's Cave release includes ménage. Two books I'll be submitting to my editors soon are also ménages, and one of those is a committed m/m/f threesome.

Right now, I'm in the middle of writing a series set at a voyeurism club that details the experiences of the characters who visit—those who enjoy it, and those who don't. I'm also in the middle of a series about an online dating website. I've written about lifelong best friends becoming lovers and about characters who are already in love, but struggling to keep the flames burning. I've written about strangers who meet under the most awkward and ironic circumstances (while the heroine's still married) and end up falling for each other. I've also explored office romances and what makes them so, so sexy! (Love office romances!)

My point in sharing the different types of stories I've written under the contemporary erotic umbrella is to illustrate how many different ways you can approach a sexy story. Just about anything can result in an erotic encounter when in the hands of a creative author. Whether it's something exotic like making love in a museum in France or as commonplace as strangers getting to know each other a lot better on a commuter train, you can take seemingly ordinary elements and make them sizzle. Opening your eyes to your environment and beginning to play with wild "what ifs" will give you more dirty inspiration than you could ever imagine!

I think I write pretty decent sex scenes (most of the time) though they aren't easy! Below are comments reviewers have shared about my books.

Regarding *Full Disclosure*, released 11/09: "...some of the steamiest sex scenes I've ever read..." Roberta, You Gotta Read Reviews

Regarding *Personal Research*, released 9/10: "I literally couldn't stop reading this book. The sex kept getting hotter and even hotter with every passing scene." Anemone, Whipped Cream Erotic Romance Reviews

Regarding *Insatiable*, released 2/11: "Cari Quinn's sex scenes are so awesome I can't even find appropriate adjectives to describe them or how I feel about them anymore." Pearl, Pearl's World of Romance

Alas, as with everything else, the reader's enjoyment of a sex scene is subjective. But here are some of the tricks I use when attempting to prod a limp sex scene back to fighting shape. These tips apply to any sort of story with love scenes and you can adjust the heat on a sliding scale.

Before I get to the tips, one more thing. Tamer love scenes still need a strong spark, even if the language is softer or the action happens more off-screen, such as in some mainstream romance or category romance. Sometimes the smallest actions become completely sexy, and I suggest watching a few of your favorite romantic movies when you're feeling stuck in that area. One of my favorites? The scene at the end of 80's classic movie *The Breakfast Club*, when Claire gives Bender one of her diamond stud earrings and folds it in his hand. Claire's a rich girl and Bender's from the wrong side of the tracks. Hot? Hell yes. For me, even the kiss they share doesn't touch the meaning and the emotion in that simple gesture.

Those are the kinds of little things you want to add to your stories to add additional layers and show the connection between your characters. Just because you're writing an erotic story doesn't mean that every sex scene is going to be an off-the-charts scorcher. Show the link between your hero and heroine (or whatever combination you have thereof) outside of bed and you'll be that much more likely to generate some serious heat between the sheets.

When it's time to up the sizzle factor...

Get them talking

There's nothing quite as sexy as witnessing two characters bare it all in bed, physically, emotionally and verbally. Whenever I can't quite make the scene between my hero and heroine feel authentic, I think about what they would say to each other when they're most intimate. Some characters are all about raw expressions of lust, others use quiet words of encouragement. Still another kind says nothing at all. What kind of characters are yours? Staying true to their voice out of bed will add even more power to an already explosive love scene.

A lot of my characters talk dirty. Actually most of them do. A good question to ask yourself when writing isn't only what your hero or heroine would say, but how exactly they'd say it. A more close-mouthed character would probably share the bare minimum when they were overcome by lust. Other more open characters might even engage in a sort of sexy Q&A with their lover. "Jenny lowered her mouth to kiss the head of his shaft, but her fever-bright eyes stayed on his. 'This is the only cock I want inside me. But right now I want it in my mouth, bumping against the back of my throat.' Her wet lips rubbed his crown, soaking up his pre-cum. 'Do you like when I swallow, Ty?'" (*Ex Appeal* by Cari Quinn, The Wild Rose Press)

So why go for dirty talk? Because I think it's sexy. It turns ME on when I'm writing, and we all know how important it is to be right there with your characters when trying to channel their feelings. Since it works for me, naturally I go for the naughty talk when I'm concerned my characters aren't connecting between the sheets.

Everyone talks in their own unique manner. They express excitement differently, they pick and choose what details to reveal, and some prefer moans to actual words. Some demand confirmation that they're getting it right and pleasing their lover. "Her inner muscles clenched around him in both entrances, and he groaned, edging in that much farther. 'Tell me you like it. All this cream pouring on my hand's telling me you do. But I want to hear you say it.'" (*Insatiable* by Cari Quinn, Loose Id)

Before I go to the next tip, I'd like to add a caveat. Some readers do not enjoy too much dialogue in love scenes. They want the deed done without discussion. Sex talk is a spice best added sparingly. You want to flavor the scene, not overpower it.

Many of us have heard the sometimes comical dialogue in adult movies. Yes, some people probably do say "give it to me!" over and over, especially when they're in the throes of passion. But things read very differently than they sound. Try reading your sex scene aloud. If some of the dialogue seems too over-the-top, consider toning it down. Or if your critique partners, beta readers or editors wonder, "who the heck says *that*?" then you may have gone overboard, especially if your previously shy accountant has suddenly turned into a screeching sex banshee, unless that's part of your characterization.

Also, what you write while in the thick of things isn't necessarily the scene you'll submit to your editor, whether at a publishing house or a freelance editor if you're self-publishing. I counted up the amount of times I used the word "pussy" in my latest manuscript last night. The total? 97. The page count of the book? 127 pages. Yes, there's a lot of sex in that book, granted, but I'll make sure I vary the language a bit before I turn in the story to my editor. But while you're writing a first draft of your sex scene, let go and get it down in all its smutty, sextastic glory and worry about possibly cleaning it up later.

Don't censor yourself as you write. My final advice on this particular tip? Write the scene true to your characters and you'll end up with one you can be proud of.

Get personal

I've heard over and over again that no two people make love the same way. Whatever their personal makeup, their fears, goals, and emotions will all be increased when you strip away the barrier of clothes.

Is your heroine someone who sees humor in every situation? Then she'll probably enjoy a good laugh when the hero has trouble getting on the condom. Or else she'll get really frustrated! Maybe your hero is a man who never stumbles in pursuit of his objectives. Yet suddenly he can't quite master the heroine's pleasure in bed. Perhaps she's taking longer than he thinks she should, or all his typical techniques aren't having their usual effect. Does the heroine get ticklish when the hero plays with her toes? Does he lose his mind when she licks his collarbone?

All these unique traits and characteristics will bring your scene to life. There is no one else on this planet just like your hero or your heroine, and their differences are what will fan the flames in your provocative scenes. Also...some of the sexiest "mental sex" takes place without ever entering the bedroom. Push your characters to the brink and they'll reciprocate when you need them to...err, produce.

This tip is also known as: don't be afraid to go *there*. That *there* is different for each author and character but sometimes we have an idea we hold back on because we think it might be too much. Trust your editors or critique partners to rein you in if need be. It's a lot easier to pull back when you've gone too far than to amp it up when you haven't gone far enough.

The nice thing about having other people read your work is that sometimes what you're writing doesn't seem far out to you when you're in the moment with your characters. And by too far out, I mean too icky, too not sexy, too much. Sometimes that's a sign you're paying attention to your characters and doing exactly what they would really do in a particular situation. And sometimes it means you're busting through your writerly comfort zones—another very good thing! In *Personal Research*, for example, the hero and heroine get it on in the hero's uncle's office chair. Yeah, might be too far. Especially when said uncle walks in and finds them afterward (though they're mostly dressed!) Interestingly enough, while writing I didn't even consider this scene might be pushing it a bit. It took my editor at Ellora's Cave to sound the alarm that this scene might be a little squicky for some people, but ultimately she allowed me to include it in my novella. "Mr. McGinty walked forward and picked up her bra. Good God, somehow it had ended up hanging off the plant stand that held her boss's prized Christmas cactus. 'What, exactly, is going on here?'" (*Personal Research* by Cari Quinn, Ellora's Cave)

Like with dirty talking, we all have a personal threshold of what's crossing the line. What I consider sexy you might think is downright unappealing. Chances are good, though, that if I think it's hot, someone else out there will too. So think carefully about how your characters would approach the scene in question and trust your gut. If you let them lead the way, rarely will they steer you wrong.

And finally... Get emotional.

The vulnerability and potential risk involved in getting naked with someone amps up the emotion to begin with, so use it. Some heroes become more aloof after sex because they're concerned about getting their heart involved. Some heroines become more aggressive because they think making the moves gives them a measure of control. It's even more fun when those roles are reversed. Maybe she's the one who freezes up and he becomes desperate to keep their affair going. Whatever your character's personal situation, exploit it. Drive up the conflict and increase the emotion until both sides are aching with the need for release.

Down and dirty, so-called emotionless sex is really hot to write and fun to read. But even strangers will be engaged in interplay much deeper than the bump and grind of body parts. Are they wary around each other because the hero knows she's still married and he's understandably worried about the repercussions of lovemaking? Is the heroine wondering if she can rock the hero's world? Delve into that. When the characters are in love, or getting there, the stakes are even higher! Use those stakes to ratchet up the anticipation level until your characters—and you—reach the breaking point.

At its core, erotica and erotic romance are about telling a story through sex. Each sexual interaction should advance the plot or reveal character nuances, or both. If your control freak characters are in bed, you can bet that they won't leave their need to dominate a situation outside the bedroom door. "'You're going to come first,' Kelly panted. Denial flared in Spencer's eyes. He looked like a valiant warrior—resolute, determined to be victorious in the battle royale of the ultimate orgasm. Coming first was both a win and a loss, and he wouldn't go down easily." (*Provoke Me* by Cari Quinn, Ellora's Cave)

Just like with my *going there* tip above, don't be afraid to wring the maximum amount of emotion out of your scenes. I've heard the good litmus test of a powerful scene is that you feel the emotion your characters do. If you're laughing, crying and squirming with them, there's a strong chance your readers will be as well.

As a reader myself, I love a story that can take me through the full spectrum of feelings. It almost seems that once you're aroused or provoked emotionally, becoming aroused in other ways is a natural result. You know how some movies and books are classified as "thrill rides"? Not all thrill rides have to be about car chases and bad guys. Let your characters experience the complete gamut of emotions (if they work with your particular story) and you'll definitely get a payoff at the end in the form of compliments from your happy readers.

In short, *go deep*. That's a pun in this case, but it refers to so much more than sex. Take your characters all the way to their limits, sexually and personally.

I hope these tips have helped you. Feel free to contact me anytime with any questions or thoughts. Good luck and happy writing!

Cari Quinn wants you to stay in touch!
Website: CariQuinn.com
Blog: cariquinn.blogspot.com
Twitter: twitter.com/cariquinn
Facebook: facebook.com/CariQuinnAuthor
Goodreads: goodreads.com/cariquinn
Email: cariquinnauthor@gmail.com

14
GETTING PUBLISHED
BY SHOSHANNA EVERS

About Shoshanna Evers:

New York Times and *USA Today* Bestselling author

Shoshanna Evers has written dozens of sexy stories, including The Man Who Holds the Whip (part of the bestselling MAKE ME anthology), Overheated, The Enslaved Trilogy, and The Pulse Trilogy (from Simon & Schuster Pocket Star).

Shoshanna Evers was listed as one of the "Most Popular Authors in Erotica" on Amazon in 2013, and one of the "Most Popular Authors in Contemporary Romance," and "Most Popular Authors in Romance" on Amazon in 2014.

Her work has been featured in Best Bondage Erotica 2012 and Best Bondage Erotica 2013, the Penguin/Berkley Heat anthology Agony/Ecstasy, and numerous erotic BDSM novellas including Chastity Belt and Punishing the Art Thief from Ellora's Cave Publishing.

She is also the cofounder of SelfPubBookCovers.com, the largest selection of one-of-a-kind, premade book covers in the world.

Shoshanna is a New York native who now lives with her family and two big dogs in Northern Idaho. She welcomes emails from readers and writers, and loves to interact on

Twitter and Facebook.

Reviewers have called Shoshanna's writing "fast paced, intense, and sexual...every naughty fantasy come to life for the reader" with stories where "the plot is fresh and the pacing excellent, the emotions...real and poignant."

When she's not writing hot sex, Shoshanna is a home-schooling stay-at-home-mom and a former syndicated advice columnist and registered nurse. A New York native, she now lives in Northern Idaho with her family and two big dogs.

Getting Published
by Shoshanna Evers

You've read all the essays in *How to Write Hot Sex* (you did, right? You didn't just skip to this part first?) so I'll assume you've got your craft in order—that by now, you've got the knowledge to write a spectacular manuscript. Now what? This essay tells you where to go after you've written the words "The End."

There are a variety of options available, but they won't all be right for you, or for a particular story. I'm going to break down exactly how getting traditionally published works, and how self-publishing works. Both are viable options.

Words to Know

Many of you reading this book are already experienced in the art of writing query letters. You know all of the Big 6 publishers (**Editorial Update:** As of November 2012 we've got the Big 5, since Random House and Penguin merged. I was hoping they'd call it Random Penguin, but they've called it Penguin Random House. Oh well.) and you've got your hearts set on a particular agent (or you're bypassing this route to go indie first).

But others may not know, so I'm going to start at the beginning, and please forgive me if you think I'm being obvious. It didn't occur to me to write about the basics first until I spoke with a friend who was interested in writing as well. As we spoke, it became clear she didn't know the difference between an agent, and editor, and a publisher. Or the difference between a NY publisher, an e-publisher, vanity publishing, and self-publishing. So I'll go through some basic terms you'll hear bandied about a lot in publishing circles.

Oh wait, you're not in any circles? Let's get you connected really quickly then. Join Twitter. Don't tell me you don't "get" Twitter. Simply put, if you are an author or are aspiring to be one, you are shooting yourself in the foot by avoiding Twitter. You don't need to have a fancy phone or be able to text (myths that kept me off Twitter for years). Just go online to www.Twitter.com and use your pen name as your Twitter handle. That way you're building name recognition every time you Tweet. I like to use TweetDeck, a free software that makes Twitter really easy to use. You can set up searches for hashtags, which are topics. On TweetDeck, I create a separate column for each of my favorite hashtags: #amwriting #amediting #amreading #askeditor #askagent #writechat and #pubwrite. Just like that, you've found other writers and authors and publishing peeps online to connect with.

Also, one thing I've heard over and over again is "I tried Twitter, but I have nothing interesting to say." No! You've got it all wrong. Twitter isn't about shouting into the Universe, it's about listening. Follow anyone you like. Follow Publisher's Weekly. Follow all the big literary agents. Follow your favorite authors—and tell them they're your favorite! We love that. Really really truly. Unlike another author who shall remain nameless, I will never complain about getting too much fan mail, LOL. When a reader reaches out to me, I literally save their email to re-read when I need a pick-me-up.

Sorry, we got off track. Where were we? Oh yes, getting yourself into some writing circles and getting into the community. The publishing world is small. We all know each other. We've all heard of each other, at least. With that in mind, try not to start drama. Don't put down anyone or talk smack. Things have a way of getting around—and words live on the internet forever. I once wrote a blog post back in 2009 saying I thought self-publishing was the worst thing an author could do to her career. In 2011, with four other publishers under my belt, I self-published and became an Amazon bestseller. I make real money with my self-published titles. But if you Google back far enough, my name is attached to an essay that is hopelessly outdated. *shrugs* At least I always knew better than to badmouth people! I don't even give bad reviews. If you look on Goodreads (oh hey, join Goodreads) you'll see I only give 5 star reviews. If I can't give a book 5 stars, I won't review it. As far as I'm concerned, if I said something bad about a book, I'm saying something to the author, to her agent, to her editor, to all of the readers who loved it, etcetera. I'm not in this business to start shit. I'm here to write. That's not a value judgment on you if you choose to go around giving books 1 star reviews, because everyone has the right to express their opinion. It's just how I choose to conduct myself online. That's how I roll, baby!

Speaking of expressing opinions, there are some great author forums online, such as Absolute Write, where you can find tons of information. Start by lurking and getting a feel for the forum and the etiquette. I've got a blog at TheWritersChallenge.com, and I have years of searchable publishing advice and author interviews to sift through, along with the actual challenge: to write 1000 words a day, every day. Don't be one of those non-writing writers. A Harlequin author once told me her success is based on BICHOK: Butt In Chair, Hands On Keyboard. That's some damn good advice right there.

Wait a minute, wasn't I about to introduce you to some important publishing terms? Here we go, in alphabetical order:

Advance: Money a publisher pays you upfront for your manuscript to be published. After you earn out your advance, you get royalties, ie more money. The average advance for a first novel is $5000. I've heard that only 1 out of 5 published books earns out its advance and starts making royalties. Most e-publishers, by the way, either don't pay advances or pay very tiny advances ($100-$200). They make up for it by paying you royalties right away. Want to know real figures about what publishers are actually paying out in terms of advances, royalties, and total earn-out? Check out Brenda Hiatt's Show Me the Money (brendahiatt.com/show-me-the-money).

Agent: a literary agent works on commission. You query them about your (completed) manuscript, and hope like hell they eventually get back to you with a request to see pages. If they love your book enough, they'll shop it around to New York (that is, the big publishing houses) and try to get an editor at one of the houses interested in buying your book. If they make the sale, the agent gets 15% of your advance and royalties for shopping it and negotiating your contract. You can't get into most of the big houses without an agent, and even if you did, you'll still need an agent to negotiate on your behalf so you don't accidentally option your firstborn son, LOL

Beta-reader: someone who reads your manuscript before you send it out into the big bad world. Someone who is not your mom or your husband. A beta-reader can provide valuable insight into what works and what doesn't work. I like to use a variety of beta-readers, listen to everything they have to say, and make changes as needed. If everyone says they didn't understand something or they hate another thing, I'll listen. But if one person loves it and the other hates it, then tie goes to the author, as Stephen King says. Oh hey, read *On Writing* by Stephen King. It may not be about hot sex, but it is fabulous.

Critique-partner: a CP is like a beta-reader but more in-depth. Usually a CP is another author, someone whose opinion you trust. You send your manuscript to your CP and make changes before sending it to any beta-readers.

Editor: this is the person your agent has lunch with so she can pitch your manuscript to the editor, and then the editor buys your book (um, hopefully) and works with you on edits. An editor can also be someone you hire to polish a manuscript before self-publishing. Usually an editor focuses on big-pictures stuff, saving typos and minor grammatical or continuity issues for the copyeditor. This is *not* an excuse to slack off on writing the best book you can. If your manuscript gets submitted to an editor looking like it actually needs editing, it won't be acquired. That's because the editor has a hundred, hell, a thousand other manuscripts sitting on her desk that are ready to go.

E-publisher: Ellora's Cave, Samhain, Carina Press, Avon

Impulse, Entangled, The Wild Rose Press, Loose Id, Ravenous Romance, Red Sage, Totally Bound, I could go on and on because there's a lot, with new ones cropping up each day. They mainly produce ebooks, although they'll also sell trade paperbacks using POD (print on demand). E-publishers acquire manuscripts, edit them, create the cover art, format them, and upload them for the author, and then pay the author royalties on the book sales. Most e-pubs pay between 25-40% royalties and no advance. Don't confuse e-publishing with self-publishing. E-publishers are similar to traditional publishers in the sense that you have a less-than-stellar shot at getting published with them due to the massive amount of queries they receive, and they have to make a time and money investment in your book that they feel will make them money.

E-reader: a device to read ebooks on. If you don't have an ereader, you can still read ebooks on your computer by downloading free ereading software such as the Kindle or Nook app, or Adobe.

KDP: Kindle Direct Publishing. This is where self-publishers go to make some serious money. Or, to sell 4 books a month (the oft-quoted average for self-pubbed authors). Whichever. Anyone can write something and upload it to the Amazon Kindle store for free using KDP. *Anyone.* Which means there's a lot of crap out there, but there's a lot of amazing books too. I've come to the point where I don't care if a book is self-published, NY published, or pubbed by one of the e-publishers. All I care is if the cover and blurb are great. If they are, I download a free sample, and if I'm hooked by the end of the sample…I can buy it with one click and be reading it in under sixty seconds. Score!

Kindle: Amazon's Kindle is my personal ereader of choice because I prefer the Amazon bookstore, although everyone has their own favorite. Kindles are an easy way to download books. My husband didn't want a Kindle because he said he didn't read enough to justify the cost. I bought him one anyway, and guess what? He carries it with him everywhere and reads all the time now. Having access to a 24/7 bookstore is heaven.

Nook: Barnes & Noble Nook is different from the Kindle in that it has color and has a touch screen. In my experience, the Nook readership has different buying habits than the Kindle readership. On Kindle, my 99 cent book sells better than my more expensive books (**2014 update:** Now my higher priced books at $4.95 sell better. Change in algorithms?). On Nook, the opposite is true—but overall sales on Nook are less than on Kindle. Way less. Not sure why, all I know is if you have an ebook, you want it on both Kindle and Nook. There are other ereaders in town, of course. Sony, Kobo, others I can't think of. But in terms of publishing platforms, I focus on Kindle and Nook and let Smashwords distribute to the others.

Nook Press: this is Barnes & Noble's publishing platform, similar to Amazon Kindle's KDP.

NY publisher: I'd never heard this term until after I sold my erotic short *The Wooden Pony* to Berkley Heat (an imprint of Penguin, one of the Big 6 (...Big 5, whatever. Mergers make a term we've bandied about for ages—ie The Big 6—obsolete.) for the Agony/Ecstasy anthology. I was at the Ellora's Cave Romanticon convention in Ohio when I found out. One of the other authors said, "Wow, now you're NY published!" Apparently this is a big deal. I had not been aware of that. Basically, in many people's minds, you're "really" published if NY wants you. At this point I think you're "really" published if people pay money for your books, however those books got there. My self-pubbed ebooks are distributed on the same page as my traditionally pubbed books and guess which I make more money with? Weird, huh. Still, I can't help but love the idea of NY, and that's why I got an agent and gave her manuscripts in addition to publishing with my e-publishers and self-publishing as well. (**2014 update:** Speaking of NY publishing, I ended up signing a six-book deal with Simon & Schuster Pocket Star in 2012, with the understanding that I could continue to self-publish. They published The Enslaved Trilogy (BDSM billionaire erotic romance), and The Pulse Trilogy (post-apocalyptic dystopian erotic romance.))

POD: print on demand. This is how e-pubs sell print

books. They don't do a huge print run and then pulp all the books that don't sell, like NY does. They create the book file, and every time a customer orders one, it gets printed (on demand!). If you self-publish, you can also offer your book in print using POD. For the love of all things holy, don't go to a vanity publisher and have tons of overpriced books printed up. You'll spend thousands and end up with a basement full of moldy books. I know several people who've done this (and by the way, this is what I used to think "self-publishing" meant).

PubIt: this is what Barnes & Noble's publishing platform, similar to Amazon Kindle's KDP, used to be called, before they rebranded it **Nook Press**. Some authors still call Nook Press "PubIt" out of habit.

Publisher: the publisher is the person or company who distributes digital or printed books. Publishers are the intermediary between the author and the reader. Unless you self-publish, in which case you, the author, is the publisher. Publishers hire editors who acquire manuscripts.

Query: a query letter is a one page business letter (or email, nowadays) that tells the agent or editor what your book is about in a paragraph or two, and then a paragraph about your writing experience. If you have no experience, you can mention any writing classes you've taken or associations you belong to, such as Romance Writers of America. Query letters are an art. If the query sucks—or rather, if the query isn't perfect—you can kiss your chances of an agent or editor requesting pages goodbye. How to write a query letter could be its own entire essay. In fact, if you Google that phrase you'll find a ton of advice. Just remember this: don't dash off a quick email with your manuscript attached and expect results. Take your time. Have beta-readers read your query. This is your first introduction to an agent or editor, and you want it to be flawless.

Royalties: the percentage of book sales the author gets paid. It's really low on print books, often like 6 or 7%. Higher on e-pubbed books: 25-40% usually. If you self-publish, you get 70% if your book is priced between $2.99 and $9.99 on

Kindle, or 35% if it's priced higher or lower. One thing to consider is you'll need to sell six times more books at the 99 cent price-point than you will at the $2.99 price point in order to make the same amount of money.

Self-publishing: when the author is the publisher. You take your own book, and do everything the publisher would normally do for you all by yourself (or farm it out for hire). You have someone that's not you edit your manuscript, and then you take care of (or pay a flat fee for help with) formatting, cover design, and uploading it to distribution outlets like Amazon Kindle, Smashwords, and Barnes & Noble Nook.

Smashwords: a distribution website that puts out your books in all formats. Readers can buy your book from Smashwords directly, and Smashwords also distributes your book to all the outlets for you.

The Big 5: (See all my little editorial updates under NY Publisher. The giants are merging and so it's not quite the Big 6 anymore.) The big six huge NY publishers have hundreds of imprints. Hachette Book Group is known mainly for its imprints Grand Central and Little, Brown and Co; HarperCollins (Avon); MacMillan Publishers (Tor and St. Martin's Press); Penguin Group (Berkley, NAL), Random House (Ballantine-Bantam-Dell), (**Editorial Update:** now it's Penguin Random House. Merged!) and Simon & Schuster (Pocket, Gallery Books, Scribner). There's also Kensington and Sourcebooks, which are independent but still huge NY publishers. And Harlequin, of course. So, there's more than six, but when publishing peeps are talking about the Big 6 (**or Big 5, in 2014**), you know they're talking about these guys and not, say, a small e-pub.

Vanity publishing: when a company charges you a lot of money to sell you a pile of overpriced books that you then have to distribute yourself. Just. Say. No. One of my son's teachers fell for this, and I felt so bad for her. When she heard I was an author, she said, "Oh wow, I'm an author too!" I said "Great! What house are you with?" She shook her head. "No, no, I'm self-published." "That's great!" I said. "How are sales?" "Well," she said, "I've sold nine books to my family and friends. But once sales pick up, I'm going to hire my son to ship them for me to the readers." "Ship...the books?" I asked, confused. Confused because you can set up an account on CreateSpace and have them print your books POD style and they ship for you, and at a reasonable cost too. "Someday I'll make back the thousands I spent," she said wistfully. OMG. Please don't let this happen to you. Please.

Okay. Here is a perfect example of why I love Twitter. I'm writing this essay, wondering what else writers want to learn about. So I asked. Within minutes, I got back a whole slew of responses. Well, my darlings, ask and ye shall receive. Remember how I said that your query letter is uber-important? I'm going to include the query letter that got me my first agent, along with exactly why I wrote what I did. I know this is a good query because almost every single agent I sent it to requested pages, and I ended up landing the agent who went on to sell seven books on my behalf. I checked out their website, doing my research before going to a panel where this agent would be speaking. At the time, I thought, hmm. Somehow I doubt they're going to want little ol' me, an erotic romance author. But when I heard this agent speak, it was clear she was actively looking to build her romance list. And so, I queried with the following email. I'm going to put my own notes to you guys in **_bold italics_** so you can see why I wrote what I did.

Dear First Name Last Name: **_Spell the name right, use the whole name. This isn't time to be cutesy or unprofessional!_**
It was great meeting you on Saturday at the NJ RWA agent/editor panel. I enjoyed chatting with you at lunch :) **_I remind her where we met, which helps make the query more personal._** I have a manuscript I'm seeking representation for, if you're interested in seeing it I'd be happy

to email you a copy (and I'll make sure it's *not* in Courier New). *This is a joke, since she made a comment on the panel about hating to read in the Courier New font. I'm showing her I'm friendly and that I was listening. But when in doubt, don't joke, because it won't always sound right.*

PROTECTING EMILY is a completed 76,000 word romance set in post-apocalyptic New York City. *I told her the name of the manuscript, the approximate computer word count, the genre, and that it's complete. FYI, it's been retitled THE PULSE.*

It's been one year since an electromagnetic pulse destroyed America's infrastructure and took down the power grid, throwing the country into a new Dark Age. *This first sentence is designed to draw her in and get her excited to hear about the book. Then I go into the blurb, which should sound a bit like back-cover copy.* Emily Rosen lives in a military camp at Grand Central Station, where women act as the soldiers' private harem, selling their bodies on the tracks for extra rations. Emily escapes Grand Central and goes on the run from the soldiers intent on killing her for the secret she's discovered—America is rebuilding outside of New York City, and everything the city's refugees have been told is a lie.

Christopher Mason, a convict who broke out of prison after the Pulse, finds Emily before the soldiers do. Mason's survived on the streets of New York City this long by looking out only for himself—but there's something about the beautiful young woman that makes her impossible to leave behind. Now Emily must convince this intimidating, magnetic stranger to be her protector and guide as they journey out of New York and into the unknown. For Mason's protection, Emily barters the only thing anyone's valued since the Pulse— her body. But sex with Mason can never be just currency—it's pure passion, and everything she desires. *I spent weeks perfecting that pitch, LOL*

This is the first book in a potential series. *Notice I'm not trying to pitch more than one book at a time to her. I just mention that it could be a series. Sure enough, after I signed with her, she requested a synopsis of the entire Pulse Trilogy.*

I write erotic romance under the pen name Shoshanna Evers. PUNISHING THE ART THIEF, GINGER SNAP, and HOLLYWOOD SPANK are available now from Ellora's Cave (published late 2010 and early 2011); CHASTITY BELT releases April 20th with Ellora's Cave. TASTE OF CANDY will be published this year by The Wild Rose Press. "The Wooden Pony", an erotic short story, will be published in December 2011 in the Berkley Heat anthology AGONY/ECSTASY. *Here I listed my publishing credits. I'm happy to say that I can now add about another ten books and anthologies with a dozen more on the way. Yeah, I've been busy.*

I'm an active member of RWA and my local chapter. At Romanticon 2010, Ellora's Cave presented me with an award for "2010 Rising Star".

Thank you for your time and consideration. I'm glad we got a chance to meet in person :)

Sincerely,

Shoshanna Evers *And that's it. I ended it by thanking her, and closed professionally.*

(**Editorial update:** Did you like my pitch for The Pulse? It's been released as a Simon & Schuster Pocket Star trilogy in 2013 and 2014!)

So that's my winning query letter. She requested the full manuscript the following day. A few weeks later, she sent me a message on Twitter, saying "I'm loving this mss. Back to you ASAP."

Then, I had a chance to meet her again a few weeks later at BEA (Book Expo America) in NYC. I was there doing a signing at the Ellora's Cave booth, and the agent came over and invited me to lunch, where she offered me representation. Whee! I've been wanting an agent since I wrote my first novel at the age of nineteen. Of course, my first book was terrible, but I didn't know that.

But wait! I hear you say. That's not fair, you were already multi-published, you already met her in person, etc etc. Please believe me when I say that ultimately, while that probably peaked her interest, it's always the book blurb that sells the query. If a manuscript is amazing, agents and editors don't care if you've never been published before.

So tweak that blurb till it shines like the top of the Chrysler Building. Yes, I know Miss Hannigan said something like that in "Annie". That's okay.

2014 Agent Update: I separated amicably from my agent after three years and seven books sold. It happens. Some authors are blessed to have one agent be the perfect fit for each stage of their career, and sometimes authors need to move forward. So if you find yourself needing something more from an agency, or if you're moving in a different direction, don't get depressed over it— it's not the end of the world!

There're a few more tidbits of advice I'd like to pass on, in no particular order.

Format your manuscript using 1 inch margins all around, double spaced Times New Roman or Courier New 12 point font, put your name and the book's title in the upper left of the page header, and the page number in the upper right corner, with no period after. Use your paragraph formatting to create 0.5 inch first line indents (never tabs! Never never. Tabs mess up formatting when the document is emailed to the agent or editor's Kindle, which it will be).

If you decide to self-publish, get a slew of beta-readers, preferably other writers you've met online who won't be afraid to rip your manuscript's guts out. Trust me when I say you'd much rather hear how awful your book is in the privacy of your inbox rather than splashed across your Amazon product page with one star reviews.

If you decide to go the traditional route and get an agent,

steel yourself for rejection. I've gotten so many rejection letters over the years I've stopped counting. But guess what? If I quit after the first (or second, or third, or...um, you get the idea) rejection, I wouldn't have become a successful author. Recently I read a self-published book called GO FOR NO by Richard Fenton & Andrea Waltz that I absolutely adored. The concept is to set a "no" quota for yourself. Tell yourself you won't rest until you collect a certain amount of rejection letters that year. I've heard of people finding their agent on the 146th try. And we all know that J.K. Rowling was rejected all over the place before she became a bestselling billionaire. What if she had given up after the tenth rejection letter?

I hope this book has been helpful to you— that the tips and advice you've gleaned from these essays will help you become a successfully self-published author. If you liked this book, I speak on behalf of all of the contributors when I say we'd really love if you'd consider leaving a review on Amazon and Barnes & Noble, or wherever you bought the book. Tell your friends.

Remember we're all in this together—there's no such thing as too many wonderful authors or too many fabulous books to read. The world is big enough for us all, which is why I created this book. Now seriously, get to work—I want to read *your* future book!

Happy writing!

Shoshanna Evers wants you to stay in touch!
Like erotic romance? Sign up for Shoshanna Evers's newsletter (ShoshannaEvers.com/blog) *to be notified when a new book releases (right side of the page!)*

Visit ShoshannaEvers.com for monthly giveaways and red-hot excerpts! Let's be BFF's!

Website: ShoshannaEvers.com
Newsletter (right side of the page!):
ShoshannaEvers.com/blog
Blog: TheWritersChallenge.com
Twitter: Twitter.com/ShoshannaEvers
Facebook: Facebook.com/shoshanna.evers
Goodreads: goodreads.com/shoshannaevers
Email: shoshannaevers@gmail.com

Shoshanna's book cover website (thousands and thousands of one-of-a-kind premade covers you can instantly customize): SelfPubBookCovers.com

COPYRIGHT INFORMATION

Introduction to How to Write Hot Sex
copyright ©2011, 2014 Shoshanna Evers

Real Ugly copyright ©2011 Cara McKenna

Five Sexy Senses to Rev Up Scenes
copyright ©2011 Desiree Holt

Boys Will Be Boys: Writing Male/Male Romance
copyright ©2011 Christine D'Abo

The Law of Attraction copyright ©2011 L.K. Below

Writing the Fine Line Between Erotica and Porn
copyright ©2010 Kate Douglas

How to Write Convincing Fetish and Niche Market Sex
copyright ©2011, 2014 Giselle Renarde

Sexy Sentences copyright ©2011 Charlotte Stein

Fighting Sex copyright ©2011 Isabo Kelly

So You Think You Can Kink?
copyright ©2011 Delphine Dryden

Biology: The Good, The Bad, & the Sex Scene
copyright ©2011 G. Jean Johnson

Rx for a Sagging Sex Scene copyright ©2011 Cari Quinn

Getting Published copyright ©2011, 2014 Shoshanna Evers

How to Write Hot Sex: Tips From Multi-Published Erotic Romance Authors

Copyright © 2011, 2014 Shoshanna Evers
All Rights Reserved.

Printed in Great Britain
by Amazon